CAMBRIDGE LIBRARY COLLECTION

Books of enduring scholarly value

Spiritualism and Esoteric Knowledge

Magic, superstition, the occult sciences and esoteric knowledge appear
regularly in the history of ideas alongside more established academic
disciplines such as philosophy, natural history and theology. Particularly
fascinating are periods of rapid scientific advances such as the Renaissance
or the nineteenth century which also see a burgeoning of interest in the
paranormal among the educated elite. This series provides primary texts and
secondary sources for social historians and cultural anthropologists working
in these areas, and all who wish for a wider understanding of the diverse
intellectual and spiritual movements that formed a backdrop to the academic
and political achievements of their day. It ranges from works on Babylonian
and Jewish magic in the ancient world, through studies of sixteenth-century
topics such as Cornelius Agrippa and the rapid spread of Rosicrucianism, to
nineteenth-century publications by Sir Walter Scott and Sir Arthur Conan
Doyle. Subjects include astrology, mesmerism, spiritualism, theosophy,
clairvoyance, and ghost-seeing, as described both by their adherents and by
sceptics.

Letters on Mesmerism

Harriet Martineau (1802–1876) was a British writer who was one of the first
social theorists to examine all aspects of a society, including class, religion,
national character and the status of women. Seriously ill in the early 1840s,
she turned to alternative remedies, and underwent a course of mesmerism,
to which she attributed her remarkable restoration to health. She published
her account of the treatment in a series of letters in the *Athenaeum* in
December 1844, and subsequently in book form, and her cure caused a
sensation, adding greatly to public interest in mesmerism. To her fury, her
doctor (and brother-in-law) T. M. Greenhow defended his own treatment
of her in a remarkably detailed account of her illness, which she regarded as
a serious breach of patient confidentiality, and his pamphlet is appended to
Martineau's work in this reissue.

Cambridge University Press has long been a pioneer in the reissuing of out-of-print titles from its own backlist, producing digital reprints of books that are still sought after by scholars and students but could not be reprinted economically using traditional technology. The Cambridge Library Collection extends this activity to a wider range of books which are still of importance to researchers and professionals, either for the source material they contain, or as landmarks in the history of their academic discipline.

Drawing from the world-renowned collections in the Cambridge University Library, and guided by the advice of experts in each subject area, Cambridge University Press is using state-of-the-art scanning machines in its own Printing House to capture the content of each book selected for inclusion. The files are processed to give a consistently clear, crisp image, and the books finished to the high quality standard for which the Press is recognised around the world. The latest print-on-demand technology ensures that the books will remain available indefinitely, and that orders for single or multiple copies can quickly be supplied.

The Cambridge Library Collection will bring back to life books of enduring scholarly value (including out-of-copyright works originally issued by other publishers) across a wide range of disciplines in the humanities and social sciences and in science and technology.

Letters on Mesmerism

Harriet Martineau

CAMBRIDGE
UNIVERSITY PRESS

CAMBRIDGE UNIVERSITY PRESS

Cambridge, New York, Melbourne, Madrid, Cape Town, Singapore,
São Paolo, Delhi, Dubai, Tokyo, Mexico City

Published in the United States of America by Cambridge University Press, New York

www.cambridge.org
Information on this title: www.cambridge.org/9781108027403

© in this compilation Cambridge University Press 2011

This edition first published 1845
This digitally printed version 2011

ISBN 978-1-108-02740-3 Paperback

LETTERS

ON

MESMERISM.

BY

HARRIET MARTINEAU.

SECOND EDITION.

LONDON:

EDWARD MOXON, DOVER STREET.

MDCCCXLV.

LONDON:
BRADBURY AND EVANS, PRINTERS, WHITEFRIARS.

PREFACE.

In the month which has elapsed since these Letters were written, so much has occurred in relation to their subject,—so much has been seen, done, and learned by myself and others,—that I am more than ever aware of the superficial character of what I have written. This does not, however, make me for a moment doubt about obeying the call for its republication. A faithful narrative of first impressions of Mesmerism, and of the state of mind required by its disclosure, is needed and desired; and I give mine accordingly.

I give it unaltered, because, first, I consider it best to reserve for meditation what I have learned within the last month; and because, next, I see no reason to suppress any part of it. The narrative of J.'s somnambulism is objected to on opposite grounds, by those who are within and those who are without the pale of mesmeric belief and knowledge. For the first it is trite,—tells nothing but what is too familiar to be worth relating; for the second it is too wonderful,—so incredible as to startle them out of their previous belief of my own

narrative. Both these representations are well founded
as facts; but not, in my opinion, as objections to my
publishing the story. They do not affect my object,—
which is not to convince A, B, and C, by what I am
telling. The convictions of A, B, and C, would not be
worth much, if they could be secured by the mere reading of a printed narrative of a single case. My aim is,
what it always is in publishing, to utter what I know
and think, secure of its reaching those whom it may
concern, and uninterested as to its reception by those
whom it does not. In the present case, this seems,
after all, the surest way of convincing A, B, and C :
for it incites many of the large number who know the
wonders of Mesmerism to avow what they know, and
thus brings out a quantity of testimony which would
still have been concealed, if I had presumed to conjecture what amount of truth can or cannot be borne by
my readers ;—a conjecture or calculation whose inso-
lence is intolerable to me even in the mere supposition.

Of the knowledge gained since these Letters were
written, no part is more striking to me than that of the
great extent of the belief and practice of Mesmerism.
I had before a vague notion that the subject filled a
large space in many enlightened minds, and formed a
strong bond of sympathy among not a few philosophical
and benevolent persons; and this impression was
strengthened by the tone of medical literature, and the
conduct of a portion of the medical profession. The

systematic disingenuousness of some Medical Journals
on this subject, and the far-fetched calumnies and
offensive assumptions with which it is the regular
practice of a large number of the Faculty to assail every
case of cure or relief by Mesmerism, looked very much
as if they were in conflict with powerful truth, and as
if they knew it. But these broad hints of the real state
of the case had not prepared me for what I now know
of the spread of Mesmerism. The last month has been,
to my Mesmerist and myself, one of hard work, of such
pressure of business as we have hardly experienced
before. But it is a joyous labour,—one which has
exhilarated our hearts and strengthened our hands, by
enabling us to counsel, guide, or at least sympathise
with the sick and suffering, and make common cause
with some of their physicians; and by opening to us
new prospects of the good to come through the association of believers in Mesmerism, hitherto scattered,
but now likely to be brought into co-operation. By
correspondence with these parties, and by the visits
and conversation of others who have come from far and
near to investigate and observe the phenomena occurring
here, we find the cause so strong, that we begin to
regard with some definiteness the means by which it
may be still further advanced.

There is a remarkable uniformity in the letters I have
received from medical gentlemen, from various parts of
the country, each believing himself almost the only one
who has ventured upon the practice of Mesmerism,

either from scientific curiosity, or from the failure in
particular instances of all other means,—each having
two or three valuable cases to report,—and each suffering under the experience or apprehension of ill-will
from his professional brethren, from the hour of his
avowing any belief in Mesmerism. Some of these have
courage to brave any consequences for themselves, and
are rewarded, I trust, by finding that people in general
are more disposed to receive the truths of Mesmerism
than is usually imagined : but, as to an avowal in print,
by the publication of their cases, the difficulties have
hitherto been too great. Besides the natural reluctance
to come forward alone, a humane and gentlemanly
feeling towards their patients keeps them silent,—
prevents their exposing their charge to the impertinences
and injurious imputations which, however despised by
all, and recognised by all as the sure tokens of a weak
cause, all have not the nerve to encounter. Now, if
these medical gentlemen knew how far they are from
being alone,—if they could be brought into mutual
communication, they might not only aid and support
each other in their study and use of this great curative
agency, but they might furnish, in concert, such an
array of facts as must command the attention of the
profession,—if not directly, indirectly through the
public demand. I privately register the names and
addresses of such as have written to me; and I am
persuaded that if these, and the many more who must
exist, could find some means of greeting each other, in

order to put their facts together, they are strong enough
to take possession of high and safe ground, and bring
the profession,—at least the rising medical generation,—
up to their own standing.

Next occurs the important consideration of the de-
ficiency of educated Mesmerists. The most painful
thought now daily forced upon us is that, while the
sufferers are so many, the Mesmerists are so few. But
observation teaches us that, in human society, the work
never waits long for the workman. In this instance
the want is very pressing,—more pressing every day ;
and this alone would indicate to us that means of supply
would soon be forthcoming ;—but we have another
assurance in the knowledge that the elements of the
supply are all abundant, and only wait to be brought
together. There is the mesmeric power,—there is the
desire for employment,—there is the heart of charity
on the one hand, and the ability and readiness to instruct on the other. Moreover, there are floating ideas
in many good heads of establishments in London where
the able and willing may resort to have their powers
tested and trained. From what has been said to me
within the last month, I have no doubt that if such an
establishment were opened,—if only half a dozen Mesmerists were to meet for mutual information, trial, and
practice,—there would presently be such an accession of
numbers and force as would meet much of the existing
need. A succession of Mesmerists and nurses would
go out from thence,—men and women of education and

of experience in their function,—who would first directly, and then as a consequence, change the aspect of half the sick-rooms of the land. That this will be done, I hope and anticipate. I should feel it an honour to aid in such an object by any means in my power.

In the *Critic* of Oct. 15, p. 121, there is an account of a proposed and commenced association for the purpose of philosophical and practical investigation of the subject, already joined by medical men, barristers, and clergymen ; their meetings to take place once a fortnight, for the communication of facts, and ideas, and arrangement of means of inquiry into new facts ;—for purposes, in short, of systematic investigation. When to this is added the one remaining instrument needed, and already in contemplation—a literary organ for the philosophical Mesmerists, the truth can hardly fail to make its way ; and the quarrel about Mesmerism will be shifted to some other ground than the early question whether it be true or not.

Such plans being afloat,—having occurred to so many minds in their isolated positions,—the question naturally occurs whether the hour has not arrived for combination. Is it not now the time for contemplative Mesmerists to communicate to each other their speculations, and for practical Mesmerists to give to the public a large number of the multitude of cases that it is known they have on their books ? Cannot some rendezvous be appointed where those who have mesmeric power, and wish to administer it, may be instructed

how best to do so? Is not this the evident occasion for instituting that work, allowed by everybody
to be urgently required,—raising the quality of the
body of sick-nurses? There is no need to enlarge here
on what sick-nurses in this country are, and on what all
agree that they ought to be; nor on the numbers of
educated and kindly-hearted women in society, who
would thankfully betake themselves to such an occupation, if an opening were provided. I never heard a
doubt expressed by any one about these things; and I
have myself no doubt that the present pressing demand
for practical Mesmerists indicates the best opening.

In reply to the host of inquirers who ask of me how
they may learn about Mesmerism, I must first say that
the immediate study of Nature is the best method.
Let them inquire where enlightened mesmeric practice
is going forward, get access to it, and study it with a
quiet and candid mind. Books are a far inferior means
of knowledge; but many can command no other; and,
in reply to the entreaties of such, I will mention a
few, not authoritatively, but because I happen to
know them, or to have heard trustworthy recommen-
dations of them.

THE ZOIST, the Quarterly publication of the London
Mesmerists, best exhibits what is done in this country.
Those who wish to know whether Mesmerism be true
or not, will find the question completely settled by this
publication.

FACTS IN MESMERISM, by Rev. C. H. Townshend.

MESMERISM AND ITS OPPONENTS, by Rev. George Sandby.

Bertrand's DU MAGNÉTISME ANIMAL EN FRANCE, et des jugemens qu'en ont porté les sociétés savantes.

Gauthier's INTRODUCTION AU MAGNÉTISME, &c. &c.

Testes' TRANSACTIONS DU MAGNÉTISME ANIMAL.

Gauthier's TRAITÉ PRATIQUE DU MAGNÉTISME ET DU SOMNAMBULISME.

Resimont's LE MAGNÉTISME ANIMAL CONSIDÉRÉ COMME MOYEN THÉRAPEUTIQUE, &c.

REVUE MAGNÉTIQUE.

These having, in their several ways, produced belief in Mesmerism, the next requisite is guidance in the practice of it. For this, no book can entirely avail; but none safer or more effectual can, I believe, be found than

Deleuze's INSTRUCTION PRATIQUE SUR LE MAGNÉ-TISME ANIMAL.

All these may be had at Baillière's, Regent Street, and with these, information about all others.

H. M.

TYNEMOUTH,
Dec. 19th.

LETTERS ON MESMERISM.

LETTER I.

November 12.

MESMERIC EXPERIENCE.

IT is important to society to know whether Mesmerism is true. The revival of its pretensions from age to
age makes the negative of this question appear so improbable, and the affirmative involves anticipations so
vast, that no testimony of a conscientious witness can be
unworthy of attention. I am now capable of affording
testimony; and all personal considerations must give
way before the social duty of imparting the facts of
which I am in possession.

Those who know Mesmerism to be true from their
own experience are now a large number; many more,
I believe, than is at all supposed by those who have not
attended to the subject. Another considerable class
consists of those who believe upon testimony: who find
it impossible not to yield credit to the long array of
cases in many books, and to the attestation of friends
whose judgment and veracity they are in the habit of
respecting. After these there remain a good many who
amuse themselves with observing some of the effects of
Mesmerism, calling them strange and unaccountable,
and then going away and thinking no more about them;
and lastly, the great majority who know nothing of the

B

matter, and are so little aware of its seriousness as to call it a " bore," or to laugh at it as nonsense or a cheat.

If nonsense, it is remarkable that those who have most patiently and deeply examined it, should be the most firmly and invariably convinced of its truth. If it is a cheat, it is no laughing matter. If large numbers of men can, age after age, be helplessly prostrated under such a delusion as this, under a wicked influence so potential over mind and body, it is one of the most mournful facts in the history of man.

For some years before June last, I was in the class of believers upon testimony. I had witnessed no mesmeric facts whatever; but I could not doubt the existence of many which were related to me without distrusting either the understanding, or the integrity, of some of the wisest and best people I knew. Nor did I find it possible to resist the evidence of books, of details of many cases of protracted bodily and mental effects. Nor, if it had been possible, could I have thought it desirable or philosophical to set up my negative ignorance of the functions of the nerves and the powers of the mind, against the positive evidence of observers and recorders of new phenomena. People do not, or ought not, to reach my years without learning that the strangeness and absolute novelty of facts attested by more than one mind is rather a presumption of their truth than the contrary, as there would be something more familiar in any devices or conceptions of men; that our researches into the powers of nature, of human nature with the rest, have as yet gone such a little way that many discoveries are yet to be looked for; and that, while we have hardly recovered from the surprise of the new lights thrown upon the functions and texture of the human frame by Harvey, Bell, and others, it is too soon to decide that there shall be no more as wonderful, and presumptuous in the extreme to predetermine what they shall or shall not be.

Such was the state of my mind on the subject of

Mesmerism six years ago, when I related a series of facts, on the testimony of five persons whom I could trust, to one whose intellect I was accustomed to look up to, though I had had occasion to see that great discoveries were received or rejected by him on other grounds than the evidence on which their pretensions rested. He threw himself back in his chair when I began my story, exclaiming, "Is it possible that you are bit by that nonsense?" On my declaring the amount of testimony on which I believed what I was telling, he declared, as he frequently did afterwards, that if he saw the incidents himself, he would not believe them; he would sooner think himself and the whole company mad than admit them. This declaration did me good; though, of course, it gave me concern. It showed me that I must keep my mind free, and must observe and decide independently, as there could be neither help nor hindrance from minds self-exiled in this way from the region of evidence. From that time till June last, I was, as I have said, a believer in Mesmerism on testimony.

The reason why I did not qualify myself for belief or disbelief on evidence was a substantial one. From the early summer of 1839, I was, till this autumn, a prisoner from illness. My recovery now, by means of mesmeric treatment alone, has given me the most thorough knowledge possible that Mesmerism is true.

This is not the place in which to give any details of disease. It will be sufficient to explain briefly, in order to render my story intelligible, that the internal disease, under which I have suffered, appears to have been coming on for many years; that after warnings of failing health, which I carelessly overlooked, I broke down, while travelling abroad, in June 1839;—that I sank lower and lower for three years after my return, and remained nearly stationary for two more, preceding last June. During these five years, I never felt wholly at ease for one single hour. I seldom had severe pain;

but never entire comfort. A besetting sickness, almost disabling me from taking food for two years, brought me very low; and, together with other evils, it confined me to a condition of almost entire stillness,—to a life passed between my bed and my sofa. It was not till after many attempts at gentle exercise that my friends agreed with me that the cost was too great for any advantage gained: and at length it was clear that even going down one flight of stairs was imprudent. From that time, I lay still ; and by means of this undisturbed quiet, and such an increase of opiates as kept down my most urgent discomforts, I passed the last two years with less suffering than the three preceding. There was, however, no favourable change in the disease. Everything was done for me that the best medical skill and science could suggest, and the most indefatigable humanity and family affection devise: but nothing could avail beyond mere alleviation. My dependence on opiates was desperate. My kind and vigilant medical friend,—the most sanguine man I know, and the most bent upon keeping his patients hopeful,—avowed to me last Christmas, and twice afterwards, that he found himself compelled to give up all hope of affecting the disease,—of doing more than keeping me up, in collateral respects, to the highest practicable point. This was no surprise to me ; for when any specific medicine is taken for above two years without affecting the disease, there is no more ground for hope in reason than in feeling. In June last, I suffered more than usual, and new measures of alleviation were resorted to. As to all the essential points of the disease, I was never lower than immediately before I made trial of Mesmerism.

If, at any time during my illness, I had been asked, with serious purpose, whether I believed there was no resource for me, I should have replied that Mesmerism might perhaps give me partial relief. I thought it right —and still think it was right—to wear out all other means first. It was not, however, for the reason that

the testimony might be thus rendered wholly unquestionable,—though I now feel my years of suffering but
a light cost for such result;—it was for a more personal
reason that I waited. Surrounded as I was by relations
and friends, who, knowing nothing of Mesmerism, regarded it as a delusion or an imposture,—tenderly
guarded and cared for as I was by those who so thought,
and who went even further than myself in deference
for the ordinary medical science and practice, it was
morally impossible for me to entertain the idea of trying
Mesmerism while any hope was cherished from other
means.

If it had not been so, there was the difficulty that I
could not move, to go in search of aid from Mesmerists;
and to bring it hither while other means were in course
of trial was out of the question. After my medical
friend's avowal of his hopelessness, however, I felt
myself not only at liberty, but in duty bound, to try, if possible, the only remaining resource for alleviation. I felt
then, and I feel now, that through all mortification of
old prejudices, and all springing up of new, nobody in
the world would undertake to say I was wrong in seeking even recovery by any harmless means, when every
other hope was given up by all: and it was not recovery
that was in my thoughts, but only solace. It never
presented itself to me as possible that disease so long
and deeply fixed could be removed ; and I was perfectly
sincere in saying, that the utmost I looked for was
release from my miserable dependence on opiates. Deep
as are my obligations to my faithful and skilful medical
friend, for a long course of humane effort on his part, no
one kindness of his has touched me so sensibly as the grace
with which he met my desire to try a means of which
he had no knowledge or opinion, and himself brought
over the Mesmerist under whom the first trial of my
susceptibility was made.

Last winter, I wrote to two friends in London,
telling them of my desire to try Mesmerism and en-

treating them to be on the watch to let me know if any
one came this way of whose aid I might avail myself.
They watched for me; and one made it a business to
gain all the information she could on my behalf; but
nothing was actually done, or seemed likely to be done,
when in June a sudden opening for the experiment was
made, without any effort of my own, and on the 22nd
I found myself, for the first time, under the hands of a
Mesmerist.

It all came about easily and naturally at last. I had
letters,—several in the course of ten days,—one relating
a case in which a surgeon, a near relative of mine, had,
to his own astonishment, operated on a person in the
mesmeric sleep without causing pain;—one from an
invalid friend, ignorant of Mesmerism, who suggested
it to me as a *pis aller ;*—and one from Mr. and Mrs.
Basil Montagu, who, supposing me an unbeliever, yet
related to me the case of Ann Vials, and earnestly pressed
upon me the expediency of a trial:—and, at the same
time, Mr. Spencer T. Hall being at Newcastle lecturing,
my medical friend went out of curiosity, was impressed
by what he saw, and came to me very full of the subject. I told him what was in my mind; and I have
said above with what a grace he met my wishes, and
immediately set about gratifying them.

At the end of four months I was, as far as my own
feelings could be any warrant, quite well. My Mesmerist and I are not so precipitate as to conclude my
disease yet extirpated, and my health established beyond
all danger of relapse; because time only can prove such
facts. We have not yet discontinued the mesmeric
treatment, and I have not re-entered upon the hurry and
bustle of the world. The case is thus not complete
enough for a professional statement. But, as I am
aware of no ailment, and am restored to the full enjoyment of active days and nights of rest, to the full use of
my powers of body and mind; and as many invalids,
still languishing in such illness as I have recovered from,

are looking to me for guidance in the pursuit of health by the same means, I think it right not to delay giving a precise statement of my own mesmeric experience, and of my observation of some different manifestations in the instance of another patient in the same house. A further reason against delay is, that it would be a pity to omit the record of some of the fresh feelings and immature ideas which attend an early experience of mesmeric influence, and which it may be an aid and comfort to novices to recognise from my record. And again, as there is no saying in regard to a subject so obscure, what is trivial and what is not, the fullest detail is likely to be the wisest; and the earlier the narrative the fuller, while better knowledge will teach us hereafter what are the non-essentials that may be dismissed.

On Saturday, June 22nd, Mr. Spencer Hall and my medical friend came, as arranged, at my worst hour of the day, between the expiration of one opiate and the taking of another. By an accident, the gentlemen were rather in a hurry,—a circumstance unfavourable to a first experiment. But result enough was obtained to encourage a further trial, though it was of a nature entirely unanticipated by me. I had no other idea than that I should either drop asleep or feel nothing. I did not drop asleep, and I did feel something very strange. Various passes were tried by Mr. Hall; the first that appeared effectual, and the most so for some time after, were passes over the head, made from behind,—passes from the forehead to the back of the head, and a little way down the spine. A very short time after these were tried, and twenty minutes from the beginning of the séance, I became sensible of an extraordinary appearance, most unexpected, and wholly unlike anything I had ever conceived of. Something seemed to diffuse itself through the atmosphere,—not like smoke, nor steam, nor haze,—but most like a clear twilight, closing in from the windows and down from the ceiling, and

in which one object after another melted away, till
scarcely anything was left visible before my wide-
open eyes.   First, the outlines of all objects were
blurred ; then a bust, standing on a pedestal in a
strong light, melted quite away ; then the opposite bust;
then the table with its gay cover, then the floor, and
the ceiling, till one small picture, high up on the opposite wall, only remained visible,—like a patch of phosphoric light. I feared to move my eyes, lest the singular
appearance should vanish ; and I cried out, " O ! deepen
it I deepen it ! " supposing this the precursor of the sleep.
It could not be deepened, however ; and when I glanced
aside from the luminous point, I found that I need not
fear the return of objects to their ordinary appearance
while the passes were continued. The busts reappeared,
ghost-like, in the dim atmosphere, like faint shadows,
except that their outlines, and the parts in the highest
relief, burned with the same phosphoric light.   The
features of one, an Isis with bent head, seemed to be
illumined by a fire on the floor, though this bust has its
back to the windows. Wherever I glanced, all outlines
were dressed in this beautiful light ; and so they have
been, at every *séance,* without exception, to this day ;
though the appearance has rather given way to drow-
siness since I left off opiates entirely.   This appearance
continued during the remaining twenty minutes before
the gentlemen were obliged to leave me.   The other
effects produced were, first, heat, oppression and sickness, and, for a few hours after, disordered stomach ;
followed, in the course of the evening, by a feeling of
lightness and relief, in which I thought I could hardly
be mistaken.

On occasions of a perfectly new experience, however,
scepticism and self-distrust are very strong.   I was
aware of this beforehand, and also, of course, of the
common sneer—that mesmeric effects are " all imagination."   When the singular appearances presented themselves, I thought to myself,—" Now, shall I ever believe

that this was all fancy? When it is gone, and when people laugh, shall I ever doubt having seen what is now as distinct to my waking eyes as the rolling waves of yonder sea, or the faces round my sofa?" I did a little doubt it in the course of the evening: I had some misgivings even so soon as that; and yet more the next morning, when it appeared like a dream.

Great was the comfort, therefore, of recognising the appearances on the second afternoon. "Now," thought I, "can I again doubt?" I did, more faintly; but, before a week was over, I was certain of the fidelity of my own senses in regard to this, and more.

There was no other agreeable experience on this second afternoon. Mr. Hall was exhausted and unwell, from having mesmerised many patients; and I was more oppressed and disordered than on the preceding day, and the disorder continued for a longer time; but again, towards night, I felt refreshed and relieved. How much of my ease was to be attributed to Mesmerism, and how much to my accustomed opiate, there was no saying, in the then uncertain state of my mind.

The next day, however, left no doubt. Mr. Hall was prevented by illness from coming over, too late to let me know. Unwilling to take my opiate while in expectation of his arrival, and too wretched to do without some resource, I rang for my maid, and asked whether she had any objection to attempt what she saw Mr. Hall do the day before. With the greatest alacrity she complied. Within one minute the twilight and phosphoric lights appeared; and in two or three more, a delicious sensation of ease spread through me,—a cool comfort, before which all pain and distress gave way, oozing out, as it were, at the soles of my feet. During that hour, and almost the whole evening, I could no more help exclaiming with pleasure than a person in torture crying out with pain. I became hungry, and ate with relish, for the first time for five years. There was no heat, oppression, or sickness during the *séance*,

nor any disorder afterwards. During the whole evening, instead of the lazy hot ease of opiates, under which
pain is felt to lie in wait, I experienced something of
the indescribable sensation of health, which I had quite
lost and forgotten. I walked about my rooms, and
was gay and talkative. Something of this relief remained till the next morning; and then there was no
reaction. I was no worse than usual; and perhaps
rather better.

Nothing is to me more unquestionable and more
striking about this influence than the absence of all
reaction. Its highest exhilaration is followed, not by
depression or exhaustion, but by a further renovation.
From the first hour to the present, I have never fallen
back a single step. Every point gained has been
steadily held. Improved composure of nerve and spirits
has followed upon every mesmeric exhilaration. I have
been spared all the weaknesses of convalescence, and
carried through all the usually formidable enterprises
of return from deep disease to health with a steadiness
and tranquillity astonishing to all witnesses. At this
time, before venturing to speak of my health as established, I believe myself more firm in nerve, more calm
and steady in mind and spirits, than at any time of my
life before. So much, in consideration of the natural
and common fear of the mesmeric influence as pernicious excitement,—as a kind of intoxication.

When Mr. Hall saw how congenial was the influence
of this new Mesmerist, he advised our going on by
ourselves, which we did till the 6th of September. I
owe much to Mr. Hall for his disinterested zeal and
kindness. He did for me all he could; and it was
much to make a beginning, and put us in the way of
proceeding.

I next procured, for guidance, Deleuze's 'Instruction Pratique sur le Magnétisme Animal.' Out of this
I directed my maid; and for some weeks we went on
pretty well. Finding my appetite and digestion suffi-

ciently improved, I left off tonics, and also the medicine
which I had taken for two years and four months, in
obedience to my doctor's hope of affecting the disease,
—though the eminent physician who saw me before
that time declared that he had " tried it in an infinite
number of such cases, and never knew it avail." I never
felt the want of these medicines, nor of others which I
afterwards discontinued. From the first week in August, I took no medicines but opiates ; and these I was
gradually reducing. These particulars are mentioned
to show how early in the experiment Mesmerism became
my sole reliance.

On four days, scattered through six weeks, our
séance was prevented by visitors or other accidents. On
these four days, the old distress and pain recurred ; but
never on the days when I was mesmerised.

From the middle of August (after I had discontinued
all medicines but opiates), the departure of the worst
pains and oppressions of my disease made me suspect
that the complaint itself,—the incurable, hopeless disease of so many years,—was reached ; and now I first
began to glance towards the thought of recovery. In
two or three weeks more, it became certain that I was
not deceived ; and the radical amendment has since
gone on, without intermission.

Another thing, however, was also becoming clear :
that more aid was necessary. My maid did for me
whatever, under my own instruction, good-will and
affection could do. But the patience and strenuous
purpose required in a case of such long and deep-seated
disease can only be looked for in an educated person, so
familiar with the practice of Mesmerism as to be able
to keep a steady eye on the end, through all delays and
doubtful incidents. And it is also important, if not
necessary, that the predominance of will should be in
the Mesmerist, not the patient. The offices of an un-
trained servant may avail perfectly in a short case,—for
the removal of sudden pain, or a brief illness ; but,

from the subordination being in the wrong party, we
found ourselves coming to a stand.

This difficulty was abolished by the kindness and
sagacity of Mr. Atkinson, who had been my adviser
throughout. He explained my position to a friend of
his—a lady, the widow of a clergyman, deeply and prac-
tically interested in Mesmerism—possessed of great
mesmeric power, and of those high qualities of mind
and heart which fortify and sanctify its influence. In
pure zeal and benevolence, this lady came to me, and
has been with me ever since. When I found myself
able to repose on the knowledge and power (mental and
moral) of my Mesmerist, the last impediments to my
progress were cleared away, and I improved accordingly.

Under her hands the visual appearances and other
immediate sensations were much the same as before;
but the experience of recovery was more rapid. I can
describe it only by saying, that I felt as if my life were fed
from day to day. The vital force infused or induced
was as clear and certain as the strength given by food
to those who are faint from hunger. I am careful to
avoid theorising at present on a subject which has not
yet furnished me with a sufficiency of facts ; but it can
hardly be called theorising to say (while silent as to the
nature of the agency) that the principle of life itself—
that principle which is antagonistic to disease—appears
to be fortified by the mesmeric influence ; and thus far
we may account for Mesmerism being no specific, but
successful through the widest range of diseases that are
not hereditary, and have not caused disorganisation. No
mistake about Mesmerism is more prevalent than the
supposition that it can avail only in nervous diseases.
The numerous cases recorded of cure of rheumatism,
dropsy, cancer, and the whole class of tumours,—cases
as distinct, and almost as numerous as those of cure of
paralysis, epilepsy, and other diseases of the brain and
nerves, must make any inquirer cautious of limiting his
anticipations and experiments by any theory of exclusive

action on the nervous system. Whether Mesmerism, and, indeed, any influence whatever, acts exclusively through the nervous system, is another question.

A few days after the arrival of my kind Mesmerist, I had my foot on the grass for the first time for four years and a half. I went down to the little garden under my windows. I never before was in the open air, after an illness of merely a week or two, without feeling more or less overpowered; but now, under the open sky, after four years and a half spent between bed and a sofa, I felt no faintness, exhaustion, or nervousness of any kind. I was somewhat haunted for a day or two by the stalks of the grass, which I had not seen growing for so long (for, well supplied as I had been with flowers, rich and rare, I had seen no grass, except from my windows); but at the time, I was as self-possessed as any walker in the place. In a day or two, I walked round the garden, then down the lane, then to the haven, and so on, till now, in two months, five miles are no fatigue to me. At first, the evidences of the extent of the disease were so clear as to make me think that I had never before fully understood how ill I had been. They disappeared, one by one; and now I feel nothing of them.

The same fortifying influence carried me through the greatest effort of all,—the final severance from opiates. What that struggle is, can be conceived only by those who have experienced, or watched it with solicitude in a case of desperate dependence on them for years. No previous reduction can bridge over the chasm which separates an opiated from the natural state. I see in my own experience a consoling promise for the diseased, and also for the intemperate, who may desire to regain a natural condition, but might fail through bodily suffering. Where the mesmeric sleep can be induced, the transition may be made comparatively easy. It appears, however, that opiates are a great hindrance to the production of the sleep; but even so, the mesmeric influ-

ence is an inestimable help, as I can testify. I gave all
my opiates to my Mesmerist, desiring her not to let me
have any on any entreaty; and during the day I scarcely
felt the want of them. Her mesmerising kept me up;
and, much more, it intercepted the distress,—obviated
the accumulation of miseries under which the unaided
sufferer is apt to sink. It enabled me to encounter every
night afresh,—acting as it does in cases of insanity,
where it is all-important to suspend the peculiar irritation—to banish the haunting idea. What further aid I
derived in this last struggle from Mesmerism in another
form, I shall mention when I detail the other case with
which my own became implicated, and in which, to
myself at least, the interest of my own has completely
merged.

It will be supposed that during the whole experiment,
I longed to enjoy the mesmeric sleep, and was on the
watch for some of the wonders which I knew to be common. The sleep never came: and except the great
marvel of restored health, I have experienced less of the
wonders than I have observed in another. Some curious particulars are, however, worth noting.

The first very striking circumstance to me, a novice,
though familiar enough to the practised, was the power
of my Mesmerist's volitions, without any co-operation
on my part. One very warm morning in August,
when everybody else was oppressed with heat, I was
shivering a little under the mesmeric influence of my
maid,—the influence, in those days, causing the sensation of cold currents running through me, from head to
foot. "This cold will not do for you, ma'am," said M.
"O!" said I, "it is fresh, and I do not mind it:" and
immediately my mind went off to something else. In a
few minutes, I was surprised by a feeling as of warm
water trickling through the channels of the late cold.
In reply to my observation, that I was warm now, M.
said, "Yes, ma'am, that is what I am doing." By inquiry and observation, it became clear to me, that her

influence was, generally speaking, composing, just in proportion to her power of willing that it should be so. When I afterwards saw, in the case I shall relate, how the volition of the Mesmerist caused immediate waking from the deepest sleep, and a supposition that the same glass of water was now wine—now porter, &c., I became too much familiarised with the effect to be as much astonished as many of my readers will doubtless be.

Another striking incident occurred in one of the earliest of my walks. My Mesmerist and I had reached a headland nearly half a mile from home, and were resting there, when she proposed to mesmerise me a little—partly to refresh me for our return, and partly to see whether any effect would be produced in a new place, and while a fresh breeze was blowing. She merely laid her hand on my forehead, and, in a minute or two the usual appearances came, assuming a strange air of novelty from the scene in which I was. After the blurring of the outlines, which made all objects more dim than the dull gray day had already made them, the phosphoric lights appeared, glorifying every rock and headland, the horizon, and all the vessels in sight. One of the dirtiest and meanest of the steam tugs in the port was passing at the time, and it was all dressed in heavenly radiance—the last object that any imagination would select as an element of a vision. Then, and often before and since, did it occur to me that if I had been a pious and very ignorant Catholic, I could not have escaped the persuasion that I had seen heavenly visions. Every glorified object before my open eyes would have been a revelation; and my Mesmerist, with the white halo round her head, and the illuminated profile, would have been a saint or an angel.

Sometimes the induced darkening has been so great, that I have seriously inquired whether the lamp was not out, when a few movements of the head convinced me that it was burning as brightly as ever. As the muscular power oozes away under the mesmeric influence, a strange inexplicable feeling ensues of the frame becoming transparent and ductile. My head has often appeared to be drawn out, to change its form, according to the traction of my Mesmerist ; and an indescribable and exceedingly agreeable sensation of transparency and lightness, through a part or the whole of the frame, has followed. Then begins the moaning, of which so much has been made, as an indication of pain. I have often moaned, and much oftener have been disposed to do so, when the sensations have been the most tranquil and agreeable. At such times, my Mesmerist has struggled not to disturb me by a laugh, when I have murmured, with a serious tone, " Here are my hands, but they have no arms to them :" " O dear ! what shall I do ? here is none of me left !" the intellect and moral powers being all the while at their strongest. Between this condition and the mesmeric sleep there is a state, transient and rare, of which I have had experience, but of which I intend to give no account. A somnambule calls it a glimmering of the lights of somnambulism and clairvoyance. To me there appears nothing like glimmering in it. The ideas that I have snatched from it, and now retain, are, of all ideas which ever visited me, the most lucid and impressive. It may be well that they are incommunicable—partly from their nature and relations, and partly from their unfitness for translation into mere words. I will only say that the condition is one of no " nervous excitement," as far as experience and outward indications can be taken as a test. Such a state of repose, of calm translucent intellectuality, I had never conceived of ; and no reaction followed, no excitement but that which is natural to every one who finds himself in possession of a great new idea.

Before leaving the narrative of my own case for that of another, widely different, I put in a claim for my experiment being considered rational. It surely was so, not only on account of my previous knowledge of facts, and of my hopelessness from any other resource, but on grounds which other sufferers may share with me ;—on the ground that though the science of medicine may be exhausted in any particular case, it does not follow that curative means are exhausted ;—on the ground of the ignorance of all men of the nature and extent of the reparative power which lies under our hand, and which is vaguely indicated by the term " Nature ;"—on the ground of the ignorance of all men regarding the very structure, and much more, the functions of the nervous system ;—and on the broad ultimate ground of our total ignorance of the principle of life,—of what it is, and where it resides, and whether it can be reached, and in any way beneficially affected by a voluntary application of human energy.

It seemed to me rational to seek a way to refreshment first, and then to health, amidst this wilderness of ignorances, rather than to lie perishing in their depths. The event seems to prove it so. The story appears to me to speak for itself. If it does not assert itself to all, —if any should, as is common in cases of restoration by Mesmerism,—try to account for the result by any means but those which are obvious, supposing a host of moral impossibilities rather than admit a plain new fact, I have no concern with such objectors or objections.

In a case of blindness cured, once upon a time, and cavilled at and denied, from hostility to the means, an answer was given which we are wont to consider sufficiently satisfactory : " One thing I know, that whereas I was blind, now I see." Those who could dispute the fact after this must be left to their doubts. They could, it is true, cast out their restored brother ; but they could not impair his joy in his new blessing, nor despoil him of his far higher privileges of belief in and allegiance to his benefactor. Thus, whenever, under the Providence which leads on our race to knowledge and power, any new blessing of healing arises, it is little to one who enjoys it what disputes are caused among observers

c

To him, the privilege is clear and substantial. Physi-
cally, having been diseased, he is now well. Intellectually, having been blind, he now sees. For the wisest
this is enough. And for those of a somewhat lower
order, who have a restless craving for human sympathy
in their recovered relish of life, there is almost a cer-
tainty that somewhere near them there exist hearts sus-
ceptible of simple faith in the unexplored powers of
nature, and minds capable of an ingenuous recognition
of plain facts, though they be new, and must wait for
a theoretical solution.

November 20.

LETTER II.

MESMERIC OBSERVATION

WHEN I entered upon my lodgings here, nearly five years ago, I was waited upon by my landlady's niece, a girl of fourteen. From that time to this, she has been under my eye; and now, at the age of nineteen, she has all the ingenuousness and conscientiousness that won my respect at first, with an increased intelligence and activity of affections. I am aware that personal confidence, such as I feel for this girl, cannot be transferred to any other mind by testimony. Still, the testimony of an inmate of the same house for so many years, as to essential points of character, must have some weight; and therefore I preface my story with it. I would add that no wonders of Mesmerism could be greater than that a person of such character, age, and position should be able, for a long succession of weeks, to do and say things, every evening, unlike her ordinary sayings and doings, to tell things out of the scope of her ordinary knowledge, and to command her countenance and demeanour, so that no fear, no mirth, no anger, no doubt, should ever once make her move a muscle, or change colour, or swerve for one instant from the consistency of her assertions and denials on matters of fact or opinion. I am certain that it is not in human nature to keep up for seven weeks, without slip or trip, a series of deceptions so multifarious; and I should say so of a perfect stranger, as confidently as I say it of this girl, whom I know to be incapable of deception, as much from the character of her intellect as of her *morale*. When it is seen, as it will be, that she has also told incidents which it is impossible she could have known by ordinary means, every person who really wishes to

c 2

study such a case, will think the present as worthy
of attention as any that can be met with, though
it offers no array of strange tricks, and few extreme
marvels.

My Mesmerist and I were taken by surprise by the
occurrence of this case. My friend's maid told her, on
the 1st of October, that J. (our subject) had been suffering so much the day before, from pain in the head,
and inflamed eye, that she (the maid) had mesmerised
her; that J. had gone off into the deep sleep in five
minutes, and had slept for twenty minutes, when her
aunt, in alarm, had desired that she should be awakened.
J. found herself not only relieved from pain, but able
to eat and sleep, and to set about her business the next
day with a relish and vigour quite unusual. My friend
saw at once what an opportunity might here offer for
improving the girl's infirm health, and for obtaining
light as to the state and management of my case, then
advancing well, but still a subject of anxiety.

J. had for six years been subject to frequent severe
pain in the left temple, and perpetually recurring in-
flammation of the eyes, with much disorder besides.
She is active and stirring in her habits, patient and
cheerful in illness, and disposed to make the least, rather
than the most, of her complaints. She had, during
these six years, been under the care of several doctors,
and was at one time a patient at the Eye Infirmary at
Newcastle; and the severe treatment she has undergone
is melancholy to think of, when most of it appears to
have been almost or entirely in vain. She herself as-
signs, in the trance, a structural defect as the cause of
her ailments, which will prevent their ever being entirely
removed; but, from the beginning of the mesmeric
treatment, her health and looks have so greatly improved, that her acquaintance in the neighbourhood
stop her to ask how it is that her appearance is so
amended. There was in her case certainly no "imagination" to begin with; for she was wholly ignorant of

Mesmerism, and had no more conception of the phenomena she was about to manifest than she has con-
sciousness of them at this moment.

This unconsciousness we have guarded with the
utmost care. We immediately resolved that, if possible,
there should be one case of which no one could honestly
say that the sleeping and waking states of mind were
mixed. Our object has been, thus far, completely
attained,—one harmless exception only having occurred.
This was when, speaking of the nature and destiny of
man, an idea which she " had heard in church " in-
truded itself among some otherwise derived, and troubled
her by the admixture. On that occasion, she remarked
afterwards, that she had been dreaming, and, she thought,
talking of the soul and the day of judgment. This is
the only instance of her retaining any trace of anything
being said or done in the trance. Her surprise on two
or three occasions, at finding herself, on awaking, in a
different chair from the one she went to sleep in, must
show her that she has walked; but we have every evidence from her reception of what we say to her, and
from her ignorance of things of which she had previously informed us, that the time of her mesmeric sleep
is afterwards an absolute blank to her. I asked her
one evening lately, when she was in the deep sleep,
what she would think of my publishing an account of
her experience with my own,—whether she should be
vexed by it. She replied that she should like it very
much : she hoped somebody would let her know of it,
and show it to her,—for, though she remembered when
asleep everything she had thought when asleep before,
she could not keep any of it till she awoke. It was all
regularly " blown away." But if it was printed, she
should know ; and she should like that.

To preserve this unconsciousness as long as possible,
we have admitted no person whatever at our *séances*,
from the first day till now, who could speak to her
on the subject. We shut out our maids at once ; and

we two have been the constant witnesses, with a visitor
now and then, to the number of about twelve iń the
whole.

It is a memorable moment when one first hears the
monosyllable, which tells that the true mesmeric trance
has begun—"Are you asleep?" "YES." It is cross-
ing the threshold of a new region of observation of
human nature. Then it goes on. "How long shall
you sleep?" "Half an hour."—"Shall you wake of
yourself, or shall I wake you?" "I shall wake of myself."—And so she did to a second, no clock or watch
being near, but the watch in my hand. For some
weeks she could always see the time, and foretell her
own waking; but of late, in manifesting some new
capabilities, she has lost much of this.

Nothing can induce her to say a word on a matter she
is not perfectly sure of. She solemnly shakes her head
saying, "I won't guess :—it won't do to guess." And
sometimes, appealingly, "I would tell you if I
could." "I 'll try to see." "I 'll do all I can," &c.
When sure of her point, nothing can move her from
her declarations. Night after night, week after week,
she sticks to her decisions, strangely enough sometimes,
as it appears to us; but we are not aware of her ever
yet having been mistaken on any point on which she
has declared herself. We ascribe this to our having
carefully kept apart the waking and sleeping ideas; for
it is rare to find somnambules whose declarations can
be at all confidently relied on. If any waking con-
sciousness is mixed up with their sleeping faculties,
they are apt to guess—to amuse their fancy, and to say
anything that they think will best please their Mesmerist. J.'s strict and uncompromising truthfulness forms
a striking contrast with the vagaries of hackneyed, and
otherwise mismanaged somnambules.

It soon became evident that one of her strongest
powers was the discernment of disease, its condition
and remedies. She cleared up her own case first, pre-

scribing for herself very fluently. It was curious to
see, on her awaking, the deference and obedience with
which she received from us the prescriptions with which
she herself had just furnished us. They succeeded;
and so did similar efforts on my behalf. I cannot here
detail the wonderful accuracy with which she related,
without any possible knowledge of my life ten and
twenty years ago, the circumstances of the origin and
progress of my ill-health, of the unavailing use of medical treatment for five years, and the operation of Mesmerism upon it of late. One little fact will serve our
present purpose better. Soon after she was first mesmerised, I was undergoing my final severance from
opiates—a serious matter to one who had depended so
long and so desperately upon them. As I have said, I
got through the day pretty well; but the nights were
intolerable, from pain and nervous irritations, which
made it impossible to rest for two minutes together.
After four such nights, I believe my Mesmerist's forti-
tude and my own would have given way together, and
we should have brought the laudanum bottle to light
again, but for the bright idea, " Let us ask J. ! " She
said at once what my sufferings had been, and declared
that I should sleep more and more by degrees, if I took
—(what was as contrary to her own ordinary ideas of
what is right and rational as to mine)—ale at dinner,
and half a wine-glass full of brandy in water at night.
I refused the prescription till reminded—" Remember,
she has never been wrong." I obeyed; the fact being
kept secret between us two, in order to try, every evening, J.'s knowledge and opinion. She always spoke
and advised, in a confident familiarity with incidents
known only to us two, and carried me steadily through
the struggle. I lost my miseries, and recovered my
sleep, night by night, till, at the end of the week, I was
quite well, without stimulant or sedative. Nothing can
be more remote from J.'s ordinary knowledge and
thought than the structure of the human body, and the

remedies for disease : and, though I was well aware how
common the exercise of this kind of insight is in somnambules—how it is used abroad as an auxiliary to
medical treatment—I was not the less surprised by the
readiness and peremptoriness with which a person, in
J.'s position, declared, and gave directions about things
which she is wholly ignorant of an hour after, and was,
during the whole of her life before.

It is almost an established opinion among some of
the wisest students of Mesmerism, that the mind of the
somnambule mirrors that of the Mesmerist. Of course,
this explains nothing of the operation of Mesmerism ;
but it is a supposition most important to be established
or disproved. One naturally wishes to find it true, as
it disposes of much that, with the hasty, passes for revelation of other unseen things than those which lie in
another person's mind. It certainly is true to a considerable extent, as is pretty clearly proved when an
ignorant child—ignorant, especially, of the Bible—dis-
courses of the Scriptures and divinity when mesmerised
by a clergyman, and of the nebulæ when mesmerised
by an astronomer ; but we have evidence in J. that this
is, though often, not universally true. I will give an
example of each :—

On Saturday, October 12, she had told us that she
now "saw the shades of things" that she wanted to
know, and that she should "soon see clearer." The
next evening, she went into a great rapture about the
"gleams" becoming brighter, so that she should soon
see all she wished.   The light came through the brain,
—not like sunlight, nor moonlight ;—"No, there is no
light on earth like this:" the knowledge she got "comes
astonishingly,—amazingly,—so pleasantly !" " How is
the mesmerising done which causes this? "—"By all
the powers at once."—"What powers ? "—"The soul,
and the mind, and the vital powers of the body." Then,
as we inquired—" The mind is not the same as the soul.
All are required in mesmerising but the mind most,

though Mesmerism is still something else."—"Those three things exist in every human being, (the soul, the mind, and the body,) separate from one another; but the faculties belonging to them are not the same in everybody; some have more, some less. The body dies, and the mind dies with it; but the soul lives after it. The soul is independent and self-existent, and therefore lives for ever. It depends upon nothing."

Here I prompted the question, "What, then, is its relation to God?" She hastily replied, "He takes care of it, to reunite it with the body at the day of judgment." Here I was forcibly and painfully struck with the incompatibility of the former and latter saying, not (as I hope it is needless to explain) from any waiting on her lips for revelations on this class of subjects, but because it was painful to find her faculties working faultily. As I felt this disappointment come over me, an expression of trouble disturbed J.'s face, so ineffably happy always during her sleep. "Stop," said she, "I am not sure about that last. All I said before was true —the real *mesmeric* truth. But I can't make out about that last: I heard it when I was awake,—I heard it in church,—that all the particles of our bodies, however they may be scattered, will be gathered together at the day of judgment; but I am not sure." And she became excited, saying that "it bothered her," what she knew and what she had heard being mixed up. Her Mesmerist dispersed that set of ideas, and she was presently happy again, talking of "the lights." This was the occasion on which some traces remained in her waking state, and she told a fellow-servant that she had been dreaming and talking about the day of judgment.

Now here her mind seemed to reflect those of both her companions, (though I was not aware of being *en rapport* with her). Her Mesmerist had it in her mind that a somnambule at Cheltenham had declared man to consist of three elements; and J.'s trouble at her own mingling of ideas from two sources seems to have been

an immediate echo of mine.   Such an incident as this
shows how watchful the reason should be over such
phenomena, and explains the rise of many pretensions
to inspiration.   It requires some self-control for the
most philosophical to look on a person of moderate
capabilities and confined education, in the attitude of
sleep, unaware of passing incidents, but speaking on
high subjects with an animated delight exceeding anything witnessed in ordinary life ;—it requires some cool-
ness and command of self to remember that what is
said may be of no authority as truth, however valuable
as manifestation.

On the next occasion, she uttered what could not
possibly be in the mind of any one of the four persons
present.   The anecdote is so inexplicable, that I should
not give it but for my conviction that it is right to
relate the most striking facts that come under my observation, positively declining to theorise.   My friend
and I have used every means of ascertaining the truth
in this instance ; and we cannot discover any chink
through which deception or mistake can have crept in,
even if the somnambule had been a stranger, instead of
one whose integrity is well known to us.

The next evening (Monday, October 14th) J. did not
come up as usual to our *séance*.   There was affliction in
the household.   An aunt (by marriage) of J.'s, Mrs. A., a
good woman I have long known, lives in a cottage at the
bottom of our garden.   Mrs. A.'s son, J.'s cousin, was
one of the crew of a vessel which was this evening re-
ported to have been wrecked near Hull.   This was all
that was known, except that the owner was gone to
Hull to see about it.   J. was about to walk to Shields
with a companion to inquire, but the night was so tem-
pestuous, and it was so evident that no news could be
obtained, that she was persuaded not to go.   But she
was too much disturbed to think of being mesmerised.
Next morning there was no news.   All day there were
flying reports,—that all hands were lost—that all were

saved—but nothing like what afterwards proved to be the truth. In the afternoon (no tidings having arrived) we went for a long drive, and took J. with us. She was with us, in another direction, till tea-time ; and then, on our return, there were still no tidings; but Mrs. A. was gone to Shields to inquire, and if letters had come, she would bring the news in the evening. J. went out on an errand, while we were at tea,—no person in the place having then any means of knowing about the wreck; and on her return, she came straight up to us for her *séance.* Two gentlemen were with us that evening, one from America, the other from the neighbourhood. I may say here, that we noted down at the moment what J. said; and that on this evening there was the additional security of my American friend repeating to me, on the instant, (on account of my deafness,) every word as it fell.

J. was presently asleep, and her Mesmerist, knowing the advantage of introducing subjects on which the mind had previously been excited, and how the inspiration follows the course of the affections, asked, as soon as the sleep was deep enough, " Can you tell us about the wreck ?" J. tranquilly replied, " Oh ! yes, they're all safe ; but the ship is all to pieces."

" Were they saved in their boat ?"

" No, that's all to pieces."

" How then ?"

" A queer boat took them off; not their boat."

" Are you sure they are all safe ?"

" Yes ; all that were on board: but there *was* a boy killed. But I don't think it is my cousin."

" At the time of the wreck ?"

" No, before the storm."

" How did it happen ?"

" By a fall."

" Down the hatchways, or how ?"

" No, he fell through the rigging, from the mast."

She presently observed, " My aunt is below, telling

them all about it, and I shall hear it when I go down."

My rooms being a selection from two houses, this "below" meant two stories lower in the next house.

She continued talking of other things for an hour longer, and before she awoke, the gentlemen were gone. After inquiring whether she was refreshed by her sleep, and whether she had dreamed, ("No,") we desired her to let us know if she heard news of the wreck ; and she promised, in all simplicity, that she would. In another quarter of an hour, up she came, all animation, to tell us that her cousin and all the crew were safe, her aunt having returned from Shields with the news. The wreck had occurred between Elsinore and Gottenberg, and the crew had been taken off by a fishing boat, after twenty-four hours spent on the wreck, their own boat having gone to pieces. She was turning away to leave the room, when she was asked,—

"So all are saved—all who left the port?"

"No, ma'am," said she, "all who were on board at the time : but they had had an accident before ;—a boy fell from the mast, and was killed on the deck."

Besides having no doubt of the rectitude of the girl, we knew that she had not seen her aunt,—the only person from whom tidings could have been obtained. But, to make all sure, I made an errand to the cottage the next morning, well knowing that the relieved mother would pour out her whole tale. My friend and I encouraged her ; and she told us how she got the news, and when she brought it to Tynemouth,—just as we knew before. "How glad they must have been to see you 'at ours'!" said I.

"O yes, ma'am:" and she declared my landlady's delight.

"And J.," said I.

"Ma'am, I did not see J.," said she, simply and rapidly, in her eagerness to tell. Then, presently,—
"They told me, ma'am, that J. was up stairs with you."

Two evenings afterwards, J. was asked, when in the sleep, whether she knew what she related to us by seeing her aunt telling the people below? to which she replied, " No; I saw the place and the people themselves,—like a vision."

Such was her own idea, whatever may be the conjectures of others.

I have too little knowledge of Mesmerism to be aware whether the more important powers of somnambulism and clairvoyance abide long in, or can be long exercised by, any individual. I have heard of several cases where the lucidity was lost after a rather short exercise; but in those cases there was room for a supposition of mismanagement. The temptation is strong to overwork a somnambule; and especially when the faculty of insight relates to diseases, and sufferers are languishing on every side. The temptation is also strong to prescribe the conditions,—to settle what the somnambule shall or shall not see or do, in order to convince oneself or somebody else, or to gratify some desire for information on a particular subject. It is hard to say who was most to blame with regard to Alexis,—the exhibitor who exposed him to the hardship of unphilosophical requirements, or the visitors who knew so little how to conduct an inquiry into the powers of Nature, as to prescribe what her manifestations should be. The "failures," in such cases, go for nothing, in the presence of one clearly new manifestation. They merely indicate that there is no reply to impertinent questions. The successes and failures together teach that the business of inquirers is to wait upon Nature, to take what she gives, and make the best they can of it, and not disown her because they cannot get from her what they have predetermined. Strongly as I was impressed by this, when reading about Alexis, from week to week last spring, I still needed a lesson myself,—a rebuke or two such as our somnambule has more than once given us here. As soon as her power of indicating and prescrib-

ing for disease was quite clear to us, we were naturally
anxious to obtain replies to a few questions of practical
importance. We expressed, I hope, no impatience at
the often repeated, " I'll try to see : but I can't make
it out yet." " I shall not get a sight of that again till
Thursday." " It's all gone :—it's all dark,—and I
shall see no more to-night." We reminded each other
of the beauty and value of her truthfulness, from which
she could not be turned aside, by any pressure of our·
eagerness. But one evening out came an expression,
which procured us a reproof which will not be lost upon
us. She was very happy in the enjoyment of some of
her favourite objects, crying out " Here come the
lights ! This *is* a beautiful light ! It is the quiet, steady,
silent light ! " And then she described other kinds, and
lastly one leaping up behind the steady light, and shining like the rays of the sun before the sun itself is
visible. When this rapture had gone on some time, she
was asked, " What is the use of these lights, if they
show us nothing of what we want ? " In a tone of
gentle remonstrance, she said earnestly, " Ah !—but
you must have patience ! "

And patience comes with experience. We soon find
that such extraordinary things drop out when least
expected, and all attempts to govern or lead the results
and the power are so vain, that we learn to wait, and
be thankful for what comes.

The first desire of every witness is to make out what
the power of the Mesmerist is, and how it acts. J.
seems to wish to discover these points ; and she also
struggles to convey what she knows upon them. She
frequently uses the act of mesmerising another person,
as soon as the sleep becomes deep ; and if not deep
enough to please her, she mesmerises herself,—using
manipulations which she can never have witnessed.
Being asked about the nature of the best mesmeric
efforts, she replied that every power of body and mind
is used, more or less, in the operation ; but that the

main thing is to desire strongly the effect to be produced. The patient should do the same.

" People may be cured who do not believe in the influence; but much more easily if they do."

" What *is* the influence? "

"It is something which the Mesmeriser throws from him; but I cannot say what."

And this was all that evening; for she observed, (truly) " It is a few minutes past the half hour; but I'll just sleep a few minutes longer."

" Shall I wake you then?"

" No, thank you; I 'll wake myself." And she woke up accordingly, in four minutes more. Another evening, " Do the minds of the Mesmerist and the patient become one? "

" Sometimes, but not often."

" Is it then that they taste, feel, &c., the same things at the same moment? "

" Yes."

" Will our minds become one? "

" 1 think not."

" What are your chief powers? "

" I like to look up, and see spiritual things. I can see diseases; and I like to see visions."

When asked repeatedly whether she could read with her eyes shut, see things behind her, &c., she has always replied that she does not like that sort of thing, and will not do it:—she likes higher things. When asked how she sees them—

" I see them, not like dreams in common sleep,—but things out of other worlds;—not the things themselves, but impressions of them. They come through my brain."

"Mesmerism composes the mind, and separates it from the common things of every day."

" Will it hurt your Mesmerist? "

" It is good for her. It exercises some powers of body and mind, which would otherwise lie dormant.

It gives her mind occupation, and leads her to search into things."

" Can the mind hear otherwise than by the ear?"

" Not naturally ; but a deaf person can hear the Mesmerist, when in the sleep ;—not anybody else, however."

" How is it that you can see without your eyes?"

" Ah ! that is a curious thing.   I have not found it out yet."—Again, when she said her time was up, but she would sleep ten minutes longer,

" Shall I leave you, and mesmerise Miss M.?"

" No: I should jump about and follow you.   I feel so queer when you go away !   The influence goes all away.—It does so when you talk with another."

" What is the influence?" &c. &c., as before.

" I have seen a many places since I was mesmerised; but they all go away when I wake.   They are like a vision,—not a common dream."

" How do you see these?   Does the influence separate soul and body?"

" No: it sets the body to rest; exalts and elevates the thinking powers."

When marking, from her attitude and expression of countenance, the eagerness of her mind, and vividness of her feelings, and when listening to the lively or solemn tones of her voice, I have often longed that she had a more copious vocabulary.   Much has probably been lost under the words "queer," "beautiful," "something," " a thing," &c., which would have been clearly conveyed by an educated person.   Yet some of her terms have surprised us, from their unsuitableness to her ordinary language ; and particularly her understanding and use of some few, now almost appropriated by Mesmerism.   On one of the earliest days of her sleep, before we had learned her mesmeric powers and habits, she was asked one evening, after a good deal of questioning,

" Does it tire you to be asked questions?"

" No."

" Will it spoil your lucidity ? "

" No."—Whereat I made a dumb sign to ask her what " lucidity" meant.

" Brightness," she instantly answered.

In the course of the day, her Mesmerist asked her carelessly, as if for present convenience, if she could tell her the meaning of the word " lucidity."

J. looked surprised, and said, " I am sure, ma'am, I don't know. I don't think I ever heard the word."

When asleep the next day, she was again asked,

" Does it hurt your lucidity to be asked many questions ? "

" When not very deep in sleep, it does."

" What is lucidity ? "

" Brightness, clearness, light shining through. I told you that yesterday."

" Have you looked for the word since ? "

" No: and I shall not know it when I am awake."

Though usually disdaining to try to read with the eyes shut, &c., she has twice written when desired — (complaining, when her eyes were fast shut, and her chair was almost in the dark, that she could not see well, meaning that there was too much light,) and once she drew a church and a ship, about as well as she might have done it with open eyes. She drew the ship in separate parts, saying that she would put them together afterwards. In this latter case, her eyes were bandaged, as she complained it was so light she could not see; and then she complained that the pencil given her would not mark, and tried to pull out the lead further, not being satisfied till her strokes were distinct.

The only time, I think, that she has spoken of her own accord, was one evening when she burst into a long story of a woman who lived in Tynemouth two hundred years ago, who made " cataplasms " for the feet of a lame monk, and cured him ; for which act he

requited her by denouncing her as a witch, and getting
her ducked in the sea, and otherwise ill-used.

" Now," said she, to her Mesmerist, " this is the
way they would have treated you then; and maybe
burnt you; but they know better now."

She explained that she once read this in a book,
" and just thought of it." At another time, she informed
us that people now think bad things of Mesmerism;
but they will understand it better, and find what a
blessing it is.

When apologising for continuing to sleep when she
knew her appointed time was up, she declared,

" I am so comfortable and so happy, I thought I
would sleep five or ten minutes longer; but it is sup-
per time; and I have to go to the shop over the way.
I should frighten people if I burst into the street
(laughing) with my eyes shut. So I 'll wake now."

" First, tell us if your speaking of other things will
prevent your telling us of diseases."

" No: it is just as it comes;—they will all come
round again."—She awoke directly.

Nothing is more obscure in our experiment with
J., and, I believe, in most mesmeric cases, than the
extent and character of the *rapport*, on which so much
depends. At first, J. certainly heard and knew nothing
of what was going on but from her Mesmerist, unless
expressly put *en rapport* with another by the Mesmerist joining their hands. But, on scattered occasions
afterwards, she heard sounds to which she was insensible in an earlier stage. A German piano, playing in
the garden, just under the window, was unheard by her,
on one of the early days of her somnambulism; while
lately, some music in the next house set her suddenly
to work to imitate all the instruments of an orchestra,
and finally the bagpipes, which she imitates *con amore*
whenever she is in a merry mood. The same music
carried her in fancy into a ball-room; and we were
favoured with the whole detail of who was there, and

with seeing at least, her dancing. On another occasion, she was disturbed and annoyed by a slight noise over head, saying that it thundered, and then that the house was coming down. What is more remarkable,—I have observed, of late, the influence of my own mind over her, while no *rapport* is purposely established between us, and she certainly hears nothing of what I say. Not only has she said things *à propos* to what I am silently thinking; but, for a succession of evenings, she awoke suddenly, and in the midst of eager talk, or of deep sleep with her eyes closed,—I being behind her chair,—on my pointing to the watch, or merely thinking determinately that it was time she was awake. As for her being awakened by the silent will of her Mesmerist, that is an experience so common, an effect so invariable, that we hardly think of recording it; but that she should ever, however irregularly, wake, for a succession of evenings, at the will of one not consciously *en rapport* with her, seems worthy of note, as unusual in mesmeric experiments.

Another incident is note-worthy in this connection. A gentleman was here one evening, who was invited in all good faith, on his declaration that he had read all that had been written on Mesmerism, knew all about it, and was philosophically curious to witness the phenomena. He is the only witness we have had who abused the privilege. I was rather surprised to see how, being put in communication with J., he wrenched her arm, and employed usage which would have been cruelly rough in her ordinary state; but I supposed it was because he "knew all about it," and found that she was insensible to his rudeness; and her insensibility was so obvious, that I hardly regretted it. At length, however, it became clear that his sole idea was (that which is the sole idea of so many who cannot conceive of what they cannot explain,) of detecting shamming; and, in pursuance of this aim, this gentleman, who "knew all about it," violated the first rule of mesmeric practice,

D 2

by suddenly and violently seizing the sleeper's arm,
without the intervention of the Mesmerist.   J. was
convulsed, and writhed in her chair.   At that moment,
and while supposing himself *en rapport* with her, he
shouted out to me that the house was on fire. Happily,
this brutal assault on her nerves failed entirely.   There
was certainly nothing congenial in the *rapport.* She made
no attempt to rise from her seat, and said nothing,—
clearly heard nothing ; and when asked what had
frightened her, said something cold had got hold of
her.   Cold indeed ! and very hard too !

One singular evidence of *rapport* between J. and her
Mesmerist I have witnessed under such unexceptionable
circumstances as to be absolutely sure of it.   When J.
was dancing, and taking this room for a ball-room, she
took her Mesmerist for her partner, allowed herself to
be conducted to a seat, &c., assuming a ball-room air,
which was amusing enough in one with her eyes sealed
up, as motionless as if they were never again to open.
Being offered refreshment, she chose some mesmerised
water, a glass of which was on the table, prepared for
me.   It seemed to exhilarate her, and she expressed
great relish of the " refreshment."   It struck us that we
would try, another evening, whether her Mesmerist's
will could affect her sense of taste.   In her absence, we
agreed that the water should be silently willed to be
sherry the next night.   To make the experiment as clear
as possible, the water was first offered to her, and a
little of it drank as water.   Then the rest was, while
still in her hands, silently willed to be sherry ; she drank
it off,—half a tumbler full—declared it very good ; but,
presently, that it made her tipsy.   What was it ? " Wine
—white wine."   And she became exceedingly merry
and voluble, but refused to rise from her chair, or dance
any more, or go down stairs, for she could not walk
steady, and should fall and spoil her face, and moreover
frighten them all below.   I afterwards asked her Mesmerist to let it be porter the next night.   J. knew

nothing of porter, it seems, but called her refreshment
"a nasty sort of beer." Of late she has ceased to know
and tell the time,—"can't see the clock-face," as she
declares. The greatest aptitude at present seems to be
for being affected by metals, and for the singular muscular rigidity producible in the mesmeric sleep.

When her arms or hands are locked in this rigidity,
no force used by any gentleman who has seen the case
can separate them; and in her waking state she has
certainly no such muscular force as could resist what
has been ineffectually used in her sleeping state. The
rigid limbs then appear like logs of wood, which might
be broken, but not bent; but a breath from her Mesmerist on what is called by some phrenologists the
muscular organ, causes the muscles to relax, the fingers
to unclose, and the limbs to fall into the attitude of
sleep. During these changes, the placid sleeping face
seems not to belong to the owner of the distorted and
rigid limbs, till these last slide into their natural positions,
and restore the apparent harmony.

Not less curious is it to see her inextricable gripe of
the steel snuffers, or the poker, detached by a silent
touch of the steel with gold. When no force can wrench
or draw the snuffers from her grasp, a gold pencil-case
or a sovereign stealthily made to touch the point of the
snuffers, causes the fingers to unclasp, and the hands to
fall. We have often put a gold watch into her hands,
and, when the gripe is firm, her Mesmerist winds the
gold chain round something of steel. In a minute or
less occurs the relaxation of the fingers, and the watch
is dropped into the hand held beneath. While grasping
these metals she sometimes complains that they have
burnt her.

She is now also becoming subject to the numbness,
the kind of insensibility which has already been proved
such a blessing to sufferers under severe pain, whether
of surgical operations or disease. It seems as if she
were going the whole round of phenomena. Where

it will end time must show; meanwhile, we have the pleasure of seeing her in continually improving health, and so sensible of the blessing as to be anxious to impart the knowledge and experience of it to others.

I have said nothing of Phrenology in connection with Mesmerism, though it is thought by those who understand both better than I do, that they are hardly separable. I have no other reason for speaking of Mesmerism by itself than that I am not qualified to give any facts or opinions on phrenological phenomena induced by Mesmerism. The only fact I have witnessed (probably because we do not know how to look for evidence) in the course of our experiment was amusing enough, but too isolated to base any statement on. J. appeared one day to be thrown into a paroxysm of order, when that organ was the part mesmerised. She was almost in a frenzy of trouble that she could not make two pocket-handkerchiefs lie flat and measure the same size; and the passion with which she arranged everything that lay awry was such as is certainly never seen in any waking person. This fit of order was curious and striking as far as it went; and this is all I am at present qualified to say.

We note that J. can tell nothing concerning any stranger; and that her insight appears clear in proportion as her affections are interested. We have tried her clairvoyance, by agreement with friends at a distance, strangers to her, and have failed, as we deserved. I hope we shall have the wisdom and self-command henceforth to prescribe nothing to a power so obscure, and, at present, beyond our dictation. We can summon and dismiss it, and may therefore contemplate it without fear. But we have no power over the nature of its manifestations. Our business, therefore, is humbly and patiently to wait for them: and, when obtained, diligently to use our reason in the study of them.

LETTER III.

SPIRIT OF INQUIRY.

I HAVE related the two cases which are absolutely known to me; and I shall refer to no more. If a few of the many who are now enjoying the results of mesmeric treatment would plainly relate exactly what they have felt and seen, putting aside all personal repugnance, and despising all imputations of egotism, &c., there would presently be more temper and more wisdom in the reception of the subject by many who have no knowledge upon it.

What should be the mind and temper of those who know the truth of Mesmerism, and of those who do not? These two classes appear to me to comprehend all : for I am not aware that any competent person has ever studied the facts without admitting their truth, under one name or another.

The celebrated French Commission of 1784, so much vaunted as the finishing foe of Mesmerism, till the Report of a second Commission, in 1831, advocated it, admitted the facts ; denying only the theory with which they were saddled. No objections that I have heard or read of, go to touch the facts,—that a large variety of diseases have been cured by mesmeric treatment,—infirmities ameliorated or removed,—surgical operations rendered painless,—and a sympathy induced between two or more persons resembling no other relation known : —that a state of somnambulism is, in many patients, producible at pleasure, in which the mind is capable of operations impossible (as far as we know) in any other conditions ; and that this state of somnambulism is usually favourable to the removal of disease, while no pernicious effects are traceable, under the ordinary prudence used in administering all the powers of nature. These facts, I believe, are denied by none who have really investigated them.

The denial met with from those who have witnessed no course of mesmeric facts needs no notice. Opinion cannot exist where the materials are wanting. Those who have gathered no such materials may believe, on adequate testimony; but they are not competent to deny. The only ground on which such denial could be pretended,—natural impossibility,—clear contradiction to the ascertained laws of nature,—does not exist in regard to the discovery of a hidden power of nature. The only deniers who can claim attention are those who have looked into Mesmerism through a range of facts.

And these deny, not the facts which are the basis of the pretensions of Mesmerism, but everything else. They see imposture (though much less than they suppose), and they very properly denounce and expose it.— They see failures, and laugh or are indignant, forgetting that a thousand failures do not in the least affect the evidence of one success in the use of a power not otherwise attainable. Putting aside all acts of pretended prevision and insight which could come within the range of chance, one act of prevision or insight stands good against any number of failures. The deniers see performances got up by itinerant Mesmerists—shows to which people are admitted for money; and they naturally express disgust; but this disgust applies not to Mesmerism, but to its abuse by the mercenary. They see manifestations, bodily and mental, which exceed all their experience and preconceptions of human powers and methods,—and even contradict them; for few of us are aware how human experience and preconception are perpetually awaiting correction and amendment from the future:—they deny the cause and the means of such manifestations,—resort to extravagant suppositions of tortured persons assuming, against all inducements, an appearance of ease and enjoyment,—of honest people becoming sudden knaves, against reason, conscience, and interest;—of ignorant people being possessed of preternatural hidden knowledge;—of scores and hundreds of children taken from the street, of simple and ignorant men and women in quiet homes, being all, invariably and without concert, found capable of such consummate acting, such command of frame and countenance, and fidelity to nature as were never equalled on the stage. They see the sick and suffering risen from the depths of disease, and enjoying health and vigour; and when it is not possible to deny the disease or the recovery (which, however, is attempted to the last moment) they give an old name to the agency,—call it Will or Imagination, and suppose they have denied Mesmerism. And so, when they see the lame walk, and the deaf hear, they talk of "predisposing causes," "efforts of Nature," and consider the matter disposed of. Extravagant theorists there are indeed connected, in more ways than one, with Mesmerism; it is a fault common on every hand; but assuredly the wildest theorists of all are they who assume many moral impossibilities in order to evade a fact before their eyes. Of the infinite ingenuity of denial all have enjoyed displays who, like me, have been raised up by Mesmerism. We all hear, from one side or another, that we were getting well a year ago, and would not exert ourselves;—that long-tried medicines began to act weeks or months after they were discontinued; that our diseases went away of themselves; that we are mistaken in believing ourselves well now; that it is not Mesmerism, but Will in the Mesmerist, and Imagination in ourselves, that has given us health. It is easy enough, if it were worth while, to answer these,—to bring evidence that we were ill at such a date, and show that we are well now;—to ask whether it is probable that in twenty or fifty cases of deep and hopeless disease, there should be " an effort of Nature," apart from Mesmerism, at the very moment that

Mesmerism is tried, and to ask what " an effort of Nature " means; to point out that if Will and Imagination can really make the deaf and dumb hear and speak, disperse dropsies, banish fever, asthma, and paralysis, absorb tumours, and cause the severance of nerve, bone, and muscle to be unfelt, we need not quarrel about words :—let these blessed results be referred to any terms you please: only, in that case, some new name must be found for the old understood functions of the Imagination and the Will.

Denial thus reaching only the means, and not the facts, it seems time for those who really pretend to a desire to know to consider what they must do next. Are they prepared with Newton's method,—to sit down patiently before the great subject, watching and waiting for knowledge to arise and come forth? Are they practised in the golden rule of inquiry, not to wish truth to be on the one side or the other? Is their temper as serious as is required by an occasion so solemn,—by an inquiry whether human beings have, in regard to each other, a health-giving, a life-reviving power, a stupendous power of volition, —a power of exciting faculties of prescience and insight, and some others too awful to be lightly named? O ! when one considers the scope of this inquiry, the solemnity of the question, whether true or false,—the laugh of the ignorant, the levity of the careless, the scorn of the prejudiced, the hardness and perversity of the intellectually proud, sound in one's ears like the babble and false mirth of a mad-house ! While we look back to Laplace, receiving all pertaining testimony from all time, and declaring to Chenevix, that, " applying to Mesmerism his own principles and formulas respecting human evidence, he could not withhold his assent to what was so strongly supported," we can but contrast with his the spirit and method of modern doctors, who undertake to prescribe the conditions of the phenomena of this mysterious power on the first occasion of their

attendance on it ; and if their precious conditions are
declined, or unfulfilled, denounce the whole as imposture or nonsense. Where Newton would have humbly
watched the manifestations of Nature, and Laplace
philosophically weighed the testimony of men, our
modern inquirers instruct Nature what she shall do to
obtain their suffrage; and, Nature not deigning to
respond, they abide by their own negative ignorance,
rather than the positive testimony of history and a
living multitude. Cuvier speaks on Mesmerism ; and
who has more title to be listened to? He says :—
"Cependant les effets obtenus sur des personnes déjà
sans connaissance avant que l'opération commençât,
ceux qui ont lieu sur les autres personnes après que
l'opération même leur a fait perdre connaissance, et
ceux que présentent les animaux, ne permettent guères
de douter que la proximité de deux corps animés dans
certaines positions et avec certains mouvements n'ait
un effet réel, indépendant de toute participation de
l'imagination d'une des deux. Il paraît assez claire-
ment aussi que ces effets sont dus à une communication
quelconque qui s'établit entre leurs systêmes nerveux."
(Anatomie Comparée, tom. ii. p. 117. "Du systême
nerveux considéré en action.") Contrast with Cuvier exa-
mining, inferring, and avowing, our London philosophers
asking for a sign : exulting if none be vouchsafed ; and
if one be given, unable to see it through the blanket of
their scepticism. One thing such inquirers have made
plain to persons a degree wiser than themselves.
Children and other superficial thinkers are puzzled at a
few passages in the gospels about belief; passages
which seem to them, if they dared say so, contrary to
all sense and reason ; those passages which tell that no
sign was given, few mighty works were done, *because of*
the unbelief of the people. To the inexperienced, this
appears precisely the reason why more signs and wonders should be given. But another passage conveys

the reason: " Having eyes they see not, having ears they hear not, neither do they understand," &c. It is a deep philosophical truth, implied in these words, and established afresh during every process of great natural discovery, that simple faith is as necessary to the perception and reception of truth as sound reason ; that intellectual pride and prejudice are as fatal to the acquisition of true knowledge as blind credulity. The very senses become false informers, the very faculties traitors, when the intellect has lost its rectitude of humility, patience, and loyalty to truth. The signs and wonders of science, like those of the great Teacher, are absolutely lost upon the insolent and sceptical, the Pharisees and Sadducees of every place and age, and should never be yielded to their requisition. They can avail at all only to the teachable ; and they can avail fully only to those who believed before.

The true spirit in which inquirers should approach the experiments of Mesmerism is suggested by Laplace's words, in relation to our subject, in his Essay on Probabilities : " Nous sommes si loin de connaître tous les agens de la nature, et leurs divers modes d'action, qu'il serait peu philosophique de nier les phénomènes, uniquement parcequ'ils sont inexplicables dans l'état actuel de nos connaissances."

There being nothing palpably absurd on the face of the subject,—only strange, unthought-of, and overwhelming to minds unaccustomed to the great ideas of Nature and Philosophy, the claims of Mesmerism to a calm and philosophical investigation are imperative. No philosopher can gainsay this ; and if I were to speak as a moralist on the responsibility of the *savans* of society to the multitude—if I were to unveil the scenes which are going forward in every town in England, from the wanton, sportive, curious, or mischievous use of this awful agency by the ignorant, we should hear no more levity in high places about Mesmerism,—no more wrangling about the old or new names by which the influence is to be called, while the influence itself is so popularly used with such fearful recklessness.

Let the *savans* really inquire, and combine to do so. Experiment is here, of course, the only means of knowledge. Instead of objecting to this, that, and the other theory, (all, probably, being objectionable enough,) let all thought of theory be put away till at least some store of varied facts is obtained under personal observation. Few individuals have the leisure, and the command of Mesmerists and patients, necessary for a sound set of experiments. Though some see reason to believe that every human being has the power of exciting, and the susceptibility of receiving, Mesmeric influence, and thus a course of experiments might seem easy enough, it is not so, any more than it is easy for us all to ascertain the composition of the atmosphere, because the air is all about us. Many and protracted conditions are necessary to a full and fair experiment, though brief and casual feats suffice to prove that " there is something in Mesmerism." Under the guidance of those who best understand the conditions,—the brave pioneers in this vast re-discovery,—let the process be begun; and let it be carried on till it is ascertained whether a sound theory can or cannot be obtained. To ask for such a theory in the first place, is an absurdity which could hardly be credited but for its commonness. " Tell me what Mesmerism is first, and next what it pretends to, and then I will attend to it," has been said to me; and is said to many others who, declaring Mesmerism to be true, have no theory as to its nature,—no conjecture as to the scope of its operations. Some ask this in ignorance; others as an evasion. Wise inquirers will not ask it at all till a vast preparatory work is achieved, which it is both unphilosophical and immoral to neglect. There are hospitals among us, where it may be ascertained whether insensibility to extreme pain can be produced.

There are sufferers in every one's neighbourhood, whose capability of recovery by Mesmerism may be tested. And in the course of such benevolent experiments the ulterior phenomena of Mesmerism will doubtless occur, if they exist as commonly as is pretended. Let experience, carefully obtained, be wisely collected and philosophically communicated. If found untrue, Mesmerism may then be " exploded,"—which it can never be by mere ignorant scorn and levity. If true, the world will be so much the better. When we consider that no physician in Europe above forty years of age when Harvey lived believed in the circulation of the blood, we shall not look for any philosophical inquiry into Mesmerism from established members of the profession, whose business it is to attend to it; but happily, the young never fail. There is always a new generation rising up to emancipate the world from the prejudices of the last, (while originating new ones;) and there are always a few disinterested, intrepid, contemplative spirits, cultivating the calm wisdom and bringing up the established convictions of the olden time, as material for the enthusiasm of the new, who may be relied on for maintaining the truth till they joyfully find that it has become too expansive for their keeping. The truth in question is safe, whether it be called Mesmerism, or by another and a better name.

LETTER IV.

SPIRIT OF CONVICTION.

IT may seem presumptuous in me to say anything
about what the temper and conduct of believers in
Mesmerism should be,—so many of them as were
bravely and benevolently enduring opposition and
injury, while I was quietly lying by, out of sight, and
unqualified to join them, though steadily sympathiz-
ing with them. But my very position may perhaps
enable me to see some considerations long left behind
by the more advanced Mesmerists, and to indicate
them for the benefit of novices, whose experience has
not yet led them up to my point of view. Besides, I
have now a very vivid experience of my own. While
sympathy in my release from pain and my recovered
enjoyment of life flows in abundantly, I still have cause
to feel, as numbers have felt before me, that no one can
sustain a Mesmeric cure with entire impunity. When
I think of the insults inflicted on many sufferers, of the
innocent and truthful beings who, after long disease
and the deprivation of a limb, have in addition to bear
the cruel imputation of being liars and cheats because
they could not say they had suffered the pains of ampu-
tation, I feel as if I, and such as I, must be for ever
dumb about such disbelief and misrepresentation as, for
our small share, we meet with. But, without saying a
word on that head, such experience may enable one to
perceive and allege the things in the conduct of the
disciples of Mesmerism, which act unfavourably on
their cause. There never was a great cause yet which
did not suffer by some or other of its friends; and while
men are imperfect and frail, thus it will ever be. And
again, there never were faithful asserters of a great

truth who were not glad to hear what are the difficulties and objections of those without—who were not
willing to listen to the representations of the most superficial of novices, who, with nothing to say but what to
them is trite, may yet revive a sense of the obstacles
which beset the entrance of the subject.

I believe there is no doubt that the greatest of all
injuries done to Mesmerism is by its itinerant advocates.   This appears to be admitted by everybody
but the itinerants themselves; and none lament the
practice so deeply as the higher order of Mesmerists.
Among the itinerants there are doubtless some honest
men, as entirely convinced of the truth of what they
teach and exhibit as the physician who refuses fees
in Mesmeric cases, and the brethren and sisters of
charity who sacrifice everything to do good by their
knowledge and power in Mesmerism.   But no man
of enlarged views, of knowledge at all adequate to
the power he wields, would venture upon the perilous
rashness of making a public exhibition of the solemn
wonders yet so new and impressive, of playing upon
the brain and nerves of human beings, exhibiting for
money on a stage states of mind and soul held too
sacred in olden times to be elicited elsewhere than
in temples, by the hands of the priests of the gods.
This sacredness still pertains to these mysterious
manifestations, as indicating secrets of human nature of
which we have only fitful glimpses.   It is true, the
blame of their desecration rests with the learned men
who ought to have shown themselves wise in relation to
a matter so serious, and to have taken the investigation
into their own hands.   It is they who are answerable
for having turned over the subject to the fanatical and
the vulgar.   It is they who have cast this jewel of
knowledge and power into the lap of the ignorant; and
no one can wonder that it is bartered for money and
notoriety.   The spectacle is a disgusting and a terrible
one,—disgusting as making a stimulating public show

of what cannot be witnessed in the quietest privacy
without emotions of awe, and the strongest disposition
to reserve ;—and, terrible as making common and
unclean that which at least at present, is sanctified by
mystery, by complete unfitness for general use. It is
urged that public exhibitions of mesmeric phenomena
attract much attention to the subject, and cause many
to become ultimately convinced, who might otherwise
have had no knowledge of the matter. This may be
true ; but what an amount of mischief is there to set off
against this ! There is much more wonder, doubt, and
disgust caused than conviction ; and the sort of conviction so originated could, on the whole, be very well
dispensed with. And there remains behind the social
calamity of a promiscuous use of the ulterior powers of
Mesmerism. When a general audience sees the thing
treated as a curious show on a stage, what wonder that
the ignorant go home and make a curious show of it
there! While the wise, in whose hands this power
should be, as the priesthood to whom scientific mysteries
are consigned by Providence, scornfully decline their
high function, who are they that snatch at it, in sport
or mischief,—and always in ignorance? School children, apprentices, thoughtless women who mean no
harm, and base men who do mean harm. Wherever
itinerant Mesmerists have been are there such as these,
throwing each other into trances, trying funny experiments, getting fortunes told, or rashly treating diseases.
It would be something gained if the honest among these
lecturers could be taught and convinced that they had
better be quiet, and let the matter alone, rather than
propagate Mesmerism by such a method. If they have
not the means of advocating Mesmerism without taking
money for it, they had better earn their bread in another
way, and be satisfied with giving their testimony and
using their powers, (as far as their knowledge goes, and
no further) gratuitously at home. The duty of those
who understand the seriousness of Mesmerism is, clearly

to discountenance and protest against all such exhibitions, to discountenance all who originate, and all who attend them, as false to the truth sought, through incompetence or worse.

The very best of the mesmeric brotherhood are liable to fall into one ever-open snare. Everybody interested in a great discovery is under a strong temptation to theorise too soon; and those who oppose or do not understand Mesmerism are for ever trying to get us to theorise prematurely. From the first day that my experiment was divulged to the present, the attempt has been renewed, till the application to me to announce a theory has become so ludicrously common, that I am in no danger of falling into the trap. I have had, not only to refuse to propose even a hypothesis, but to guard my language so carefully as that by no pretence of an inference could any be ascribed to me. I could wish that all who, like myself, know personally but a few facts, (however clear,) were as careful about this as the occasion requires. Their notions of a transmission of a fluid, electric or other;—of a conditional excitement in human beings of a power of control or stimulus of their own vital functions;—of the mesmeric power residing in the Will of the Mesmerist, or in the Imagination or Will of the patient; of some sympathetic function, express but obscure, and assigned to some unexplored region of the brain,—these notions, and many more, may each suit the phenomena which have come under the notice of the expounders; but no one of them will hold good with all the facts that are established. The phenomena are so various, that it seems to me most improbable that we can yet be near the true theory ; to say nothing of what is very obvious—that the suppositions offered are little but words. It would be time enough to show this, if the hypotheses would fit; but they do not. What becomes of the transmission of fluid when the Mesmerist acts, without concert, on a patient a hundred miles off? What becomes of the patient's power of Ima-

gination when he is mesmerised unconsciously? and of
the operator's power of Will when the Mesmerist is un-
informed and obedient, acting in the dark, under the
directions of the patient? and so on, through the whole
array of theories. Now, it happens every day, that
when objectors overthrow an offered theory, they are
held by themselves, and everybody else but the really
philosophical, to have overthrown the subject to which
it relates. Thus is Mesmerism perpetually, as people
say, overthrown ; and though it is sure to be soon found
standing, as it was before, on its basis of facts, and daily
strengthened by new facts, yet it is obscured for the
moment by every passing fog of false reasoning that is
allowed to envelope it.

Much mischief is done by a rash and hasty zeal in
undertaking cases of sickness or infirmity. Some of the
most earnest believers, anxious to afford proof to others,
lay their hands on sick or well, without duly considering
whether they have health and power of body and mind,
command of time, patience and means, and of such
knowledge as will obviate hesitation and flagging, and
consequent failure in the treatment. This is far too
light a use to be made of a power sacred to higher purposes than those of curiosity or mere assertion. And
there cannot be too serious a preparation for its purer
and higher use—in the cure of disease. Ill-qualified
agents are not permitted to administer any other great
natural power ; and why should we permit ourselves to
administer this influence—to undertake to infuse health,
to feed the vital principle, accepting any manifestations
that may occur by the way, unless we know ourselves to
be so strong in body and mind, so free from infirmity, so
able to command leisure, as that we may reasonably hope
that the fountain of our influence will not intermit? Per-
suasives to courage are little needed, for the sight of
suffering inspires believers in Mesmerism with an almost
irresistible desire to relieve the sick. There is abundance
of benevolent impulse. What we want to make sure of

is, calm foresight in undertaking serious cases, and
strenuousness of patience in carrying them on; and,
moreover, a steady refusal to lay hands on sick or well
for purposes of amusement, or victory over unbelievers.
These conditions being secured, I believe Mesmerism to
be invariably favourable in its operation, where it acts
at all. I never heard of any harm being done by it,
where as much prudence was employed as we apply in
the use of fire, water, and food.

I will say little on one head, of which much is
said to me—the tendency of the early holders of any
discovery, or re-discovery, to overrate its influence on
human affairs. The tendency is natural and common
enough; and time alone can prove whether there is folly
in the believers in Mesmerism being so excited and
engrossed as they are by what they see and learn. I
am in too early a stage of the investigation to be able to
say anything that ought to be of weight on this head.
I can only declare, while knowing myself to be in as
calm, quiet, and serious a state of nerves and mind as I
am capable of being, that I think it a mistake to say
that Mesmerism will become merely one among a thousand curative means, and that it will not produce any
practical changes in the mutual relations of human
beings. From what I have witnessed of the power of
mind over body, and of mind over mind, and from what
I have experienced of the exercise of the inner faculties
under the operation of Mesmerism, I am persuaded that
immense and inestimable changes will take place in the
scope and destiny of the individual human being on
earth, and in the relations of all. If it were proposed as
an abstract question, every one would admit that the
human lot on earth might and must be incalculably
altered by the bestowment on human beings of a new
faculty, and also by such an exaltation of any existing
faculty as must entirely change its scope and operation.
The case is the same, if any occult inherent faculty
becomes reachable—educible; and there are not a few

subjects of Mesmerism who know that either this is the case, or that an existing faculty is exalted above their own recognition. Of these, I am one. We do not expect credence when we say this; for, by the very conditions of the experience, it is incommunicable. It is no help to the communication to be met by the strongest faith and sympathy; for the very means of communication are absent. The language which might convey it does not exist; and the effort to explain ourselves is as useless and hopeless as for the born blind and deaf to impart to each other an experience of sounds and colours. Let me add, that it would be as reasonable for these blind and deaf to question each others' wits as for any who have never been mesmerised to doubt the sanity of those who come, calm and healthful, out of an experience of its ulterior states. My own conviction is, that when that region is purely attained, it is, and ever will be, found clear of all absurdities, delusions, and perturbations, where the faculties may enjoy their highest health and exercise. I make this avowal of what can never be substantiated in my favour for a practical object—that some one or more may be led to reflect on the origin of spurious claims to divine inspiration, such as have, through all time, arisen in the world. If any one thoughtful mind is led on to a better solution than the universal suppositions of madness and imposture, there is so much the more hope that pretensions to divine inspiration will be transmuted into something more true, and that much madness and imposture hitherto consequent on such pretensions may die out. I care nothing for any precipitate conclusions of the unaccustomed to such researches, in regard to my own wits, if I can lead one informed and philosophical intellect to consider afresh how little we yet comprehend of the words we are so often repeating, " We are fearfully and wonderfully made."

From a point of contemplation like this, can it be needful to glance aside at our danger of bearing our-

selves unworthily amidst the irritations of opposition
and scorn that we have to encounter? It is most needful to do more than glance at this danger—to regard it
steadily. If we firmly hold our convictions, we cannot
at all times maintain, without an effort, the high ground
on which they place us. It is new and painful to us
to have our statements discredited to our faces—our
understandings despised—some of our deepest senti-
ments and most solemnly-acquired knowledge made a
jest of. Perhaps it is more painful still to find the
facts for which we are the authorities twisted and mis-
represented, instead of denied, and one of the most
serious subjects that ever has occupied, or can occupy,
the attention of mankind treated with a levity which,
though we know it to be mere ignorance, is to us
profaneness. I say "we" in this connexion, though
I have met with less than my fair proportion of this
kind of trial, owing to previous circumstances, which
have no connexion with my present testimony. I say
" we," because I wish to cast in my lot with my fellow-
believers for the pains and penalties of faith in Mesmerism which yet remain, if indeed I may be permitted
the honour of sharing them with the earlier confessors,
who have suffered and sacrificed more in the cause than
now remains to be suffered and sacrificed by any number of later disciples. I say " we," also, because I
need, as much as any one, plain monitions as to the
spirit in which the truths of Mesmerism ought to be
held.

Seeing, as we do at times, how many there are who
cannot believe in anything so out of their way—how
many who *cannot* see what is before their eyes, or hear
what meets their ears, or understand what offers itself to
their understandings, through preconceptions and nar-
row and rigid habits of mind—how many who *cannot*
retain the convictions of the hour, but go home and
shake them all out of their minds on the way, or throw
them overboard at the first jest they hear—how the

cold and passionless pass through life without any sense
of its commonest, but deepest and highest mysteries;—
knowing these things in our soberest moments, why
cannot we bear them about with us amidst the opposi-
tions we meet with in society?   Why should we chafe
ourselves because minds are not all of the same rank
and quality, or interested in the same pursuits—as if
truth could not wait to be apprehended, and privilege to
be accepted?   On behalf of the sick and mutilated,
who, in addition to their pain and infirmity, have to bear
insult and calumny, some indignation may be allowed;
but for ourselves, we should be at once too humble
and too proud to entertain it: too humble on the
ground of our exceedingly imperfect knowledge, and
too highly graced by our privilege of such knowledge
as we have to deprecate the displeasure of others at
our use of it.   Though I have had more cause for
grateful surprise at the candour and sympathy I have
met with, than for regret at short-comings of temper
among my friends, there was a season when the following words, in a letter from a friend (one who was
restored to health through Mesmerism, when such an
experience involved much more moral suffering than
now), went to my heart with most affecting force:—
" Is it needless (if so, forgive me) to beg you to seek
patience when you find people will disbelieve their own
eyes and ears?   My experience is not less close or
heartfelt than yours, though I had not to be relieved
from actual pain.   At first, it made tears come to my
heart when others were not grateful in my way for my
cure; and rather indignant was I too when they doubted
my statements; but do not you be like what I was.
[Would I were!]   Why should we be believed more
than those of old, who were disbelieved? and do not
men act according to their natures?   Is there childlike faith on the earth, any more in these than in former days?   If there were, would not —— and ——
have believed even poor honest me?"

A postscript to this letter carries us on to the thought of our privileges :—" I observe that you see and feel the *beauty* which it is useless to talk of to unbelievers." Yes, indeed ! and when the word " compensation " rises to my lips, I put it down as an expression of ingratitude, — so little proportion can our vexations bear to our gains—so insignificant is this sprinkling of tares amidst the harvest to which we are putting our hands.

Perhaps it is better not to enter upon any account of what it is to see the purest human ministering that can be beheld—a ministering which has all affection, and no instinct in it—where the power follows the course of the affections, and proceeds with them " from strength to strength," the benevolence invigorated by its own good deeds, and invigorating in its turn the benign influence. Time, and a wise and principled use of this yet obscure power, will show how far it can go in spreading among the human family a beneficent and uniting ministration, by which a singularly close spiritual sympathy, enlightened and guarded by insight, may be attained. There is moral beauty, acting through physical amelioration, in the means, and the extremest conceivable moral beauty in the anticipated end. To witness and contemplate these means and this end is a privilege better indicated than expatiated on. Such brethren and sisters of charity as the world has yet known have won the reverence and affection of all hearts. There is beauty in the spectacle and contemplation of a new and higher order of these arising, to achieve, with equal devotedness, a more efficacious and a more elevated labour of love and piety.

A consideration more clearly open to general sympathy (at least, the general sympathy of the wise) is, that, through all time, the privilege rests with the believers, and not with those who, for any cause, cannot enter into new truth. Affirmative conviction is, here, as we may suppose it may be hereafter, the chief of blessings, and the securest, when it is reached at once through the unclouded reason and the ingenuous heart. The possession of this blessing has oftentimes been found a treasure, for which it was easy to lose the whole world, and possible to meet persecution, isolation, the consuming of the body, and the racking of the affections, with steadiness and serenity. What ought now, then, to be complained of as the natural cost of our portion of this blessing? Complaint, regret, is not to be thought of. To know certainly any new thing of human nature, to believe firmly any great purpose of human destiny, is a privilege so inestimable, adds such a value to the individual life of each of us, such a sacredness to collective human existence, that the liabilities to which it subjects us should pervert our minds no more than motes should distort the sunbeams.

Tynemouth, Nov. **28, 1844.**

LETTER V.

FREEDOM OF ACCEPTANCE.

MANY persons suppose that when the truth, use, and beauty of Mesmerism are established, all is settled; that no further ground remains for a rejection of it. My own late experience, and my observation of what is passing abroad, convince me that this is a mistake. I know that there are many who admit the truth and function of Mesmerism, who yet discountenance it. I know that the repudiation of it is far more extensive than the denial. It gives me pain to hear this fact made the occasion of contemptuous remark, as it is too often, by such as know Mesmerism to be true. The repudiation I speak of proceeds from minds of a high order; and their superstition (if superstition it be) should be encountered with better weapons than the arrogant compassion which I have heard expressed.

I own I have less sympathy with those who throw down their facts before the world, and then despise all who will not be in haste to take them up, than with some I know of, who would seriously rather suffer to any extent, than have recourse to relief which they believe unauthorised; who would rather that a mystery remained sacred than have it divulged for their own benefit; who tell me to my face that they would rather see me sent back to my couch of pain than witness any tampering with the hidden things of Providence. There is a sublime rectitude of sentiment here, which commands and wins one's reverence and sympathy; and if the facts of the history and condition of Mesmerism would bear out the sentiment, no one would more cordially respond to it than I—no one would have been more scrupulous about procuring recovery by such means—no one would have recoiled with more fear and disgust from the work of making known what I have experienced and learned. But I am persuaded that a knowledge of existing facts clears up the duty of the case, so as to prove that the sentiment must, while preserving all its veneration and tenderness, take a new direction, for the honour of God and the safety of man.

Granting to all who wish that the powers and practice of Mesmerism (for which a better name is sadly wanted) are as old as man and society; that from age to age there have been endowments and functions sacred from popular use, and therefore committed by providential authority to the hands of a sacred class; that the existence of mysteries ever has been, and probably must ever be, essential to the spiritual welfare of man; that there should ever be a powerful sentiment of sanctity investing the subject of the ulterior powers of immortal beings in their mortal state; that it is extremely awful to witness, and much more to elicit, hidden faculties, and to penetrate by their agency into regions of knowledge otherwise unattainable:—admitting all these things, still the facts of the present condition of Mesmerism in this country, and on two continents, leave, to those who know them, no doubt of the folly and sin of turning away from the study of the subject. It is no matter of choice whether the subject shall remain sacred—a deposit of mystery in the hands of the Church—as it was in the Middle Ages, and as the Pope and many Protestants would have it still. The Pope has issued an edict against the study and practice of Mesmerism in his dominions; and there are some members of the Church of England who would have the same suppression attempted by means of ecclesiastical and civil law at home. But for this it is too late: the knowledge and practice are all abroad in society; and they are no more to be reclaimed than the waters, when out in floods, can be gathered back into reservoirs. The only effect of such prohibitions would be to deter from the study of Mesmerism the very class who should assume its administration, and to drive disease, compassion, and curiosity into holes and corners to practise as a sin what is now done openly and guiltlessly, however recklessly, through an ignorance for which the educated are responsible. The time is past for facts of natural philosophy to be held at discretion by priesthoods ; for any facts which concern all human beings to be a deposit in the hands of any social class. Instead of re-enacting the scenes of old—setting up temples with secret chambers, oracles, and miraculous ministrations—instead of reviving the factitious sin and cruel penalties of witchcraft, (all forms assumed by mesmeric powers and faculties in different times), instead of exhibiting false mysteries in an age of investigation, it is clearly our business to strip false mysteries of their falseness, in order to secure due reverence to the true, of which there will ever be no lack.   Mystery can never fail while man is finite : his highest faculties of faith will, through all time and all eternity, find ample exercise in waiting on truths above his ken : there will ever be in advance of the human soul a region "dark through excess of light ;" while all labour spent on surrounding clear facts with artificial mystery is just so much profane effort spent in drawing minds away from the genuine objects of faith.   And look at the consequences ! Because philosophers will not study the facts of that mental *rapport* which takes place in Mesmerism, whereby the mind of the ignorant often gives out in echo the knowledge of the informed, we have claims of inspiration springing up right and left.   Because medical men will not study the facts of the mesmeric trance, nor ascertain the extremest of its singularities, we have tales of Estaticas, and of sane men going into the Tyrol and elsewhere to contemplate, as a sign from heaven, what their physicians ought to be able to report of at home as

natural phenomena easily producible in certain states of
disease. Because physiologists and mental philosophers
will not attend to facts from whose vastness they pusilla-
nimously shrink, the infinitely delicate mechanism and
organisation of brain, nerves and mind are thrown as a
toy into the hands of children and other ignorant persons, and of the base. What, again, can follow from
this but the desecration, in the eyes of the many, of
things which ought to command their reverence? What
becomes of really divine inspiration when the commonest
people find they can elicit marvels of prevision and
insight? What becomes of the veneration for religious
contemplation when Estaticas are found to be at the
command of very unhallowed—wholly unauthorised
hands? What becomes of the respect in which the
medical profession ought to be held, when the friends
of the sick and suffering, with their feelings all alive,
see the doctors' skill and science overborne and set
aside by means at the command of an ignorant neigh-
bour,—means which are all ease and pleasantness?
How can the profession hold its dominion over minds,
however backed by law and the opinion of the educated, when the vulgar see and know that limbs are
removed without pain, in opposition to the will of
doctors, and in spite of their denial of the facts? What
avails the decision of a whole College of Surgeons that
such a thing could not be, when a whole town full of
people know that it was? Which must succumb, the
learned body or the fact? Thus are objects of reverence desecrated, not sanctified, by attempted restriction
of truth, or of research into it. Thus are human passions and human destinies committed to reckless hands,
for sport or abuse. No wonder if somnambules are
made into fortune-tellers,—no wonder if they are made
into prophets of fear, malice, and revenge, by reflecting
in their somnambulism the fear, malice, and revenge of
their questioners;—no wonder if they are made even
ministers of death, by being led from sick-bed to sick-

bed in the dim and dreary alleys of our towns, to declare
which of the sick will recover, and which will die! Does
any one suppose that powers so popular, and now so
diffused, can be interdicted by law, — such oracles
silenced by the reserve of the squeamish,—such appeals
to human passions hushed, in an age of universal communication, by the choice of a class or two to be themselves dumb? No: this is not the way. It is terribly
late to be setting about choosing a way, but something
must be done; and that something is clearly for those
whose studies and art relate to the human frame to take
up, earnestly and avowedly, the investigation of this
weighty matter;—to take its practice into their own
hands, in virtue of the irresistible claim of qualification.
When they become the wisest and the most skilful in
the administration of Mesmerism, others, even the most
reckless vulgar, will no more think of interfering than
they now do of using the lancet, or operating on the
eye. Here, as elsewhere, knowledge is power. The
greater knowledge will ever insure the superior power.
At present, the knowledge of Mesmerism, superficial
and scanty as it is, is out of the professional pale. When
it is excelled by that which issues from within the professional pale, the remedial and authoritative power will
reside where it ought; and not till then. These are the
chief considerations which have caused me to put forth
these letters in the *Athenæum;*—an act which may seem
rash to all who are unaware of the extent of the popular
knowledge and practice of Mesmerism. The *Athenæum*
is not likely to reach the ignorant classes of our towns;
and if it did, the cases I have related would be less
striking to them than numbers they have learned by
the means of itinerant Mesmerists. The *Athenæum*
does reach large numbers of educated and professional
men; and I trust some of them may possibly be aroused
to consideration of the part it behoves them to take.

As for the frequent objection brought against inquiry
into Mesmerism, that there should be no countenance

of an influence which gives human beings such power over one another, I really think a moment's reflection, and a very slight knowledge of Mesmerism, would supply both the answers which the objection requires. First, it is too late, as I have said above; the power is abroad, and ought to be guided and controlled. Next, this is but one addition to the powers we have over one another already; and a far more slow and difficult one than many which are safely enough possessed. Every apothecary's shop is full of deadly drugs—every work-shop is full of deadly weapons—wherever we go, there are plenty of people who could knock us down, rob and murder us; wherever we live, there are plenty of people who could defame and ruin us. Why do they not? Because moral considerations deter them. Then bring the same moral considerations to bear on the subject of Mesmerism. If the fear is of laying victims prostrate in trance, and exercising spells over them, the answer is, that this is done with infinitely greater ease and cer-tainty by drugs than it can ever be by Mesmerism; by drugs which are to be had in every street. And as sensible people do not let narcotic drugs lie about in their houses, within reach of the ignorant and mischiev-ous, so would they see that Mesmerism was not prac-tised without witnesses and proper superintendence. It is a mistake, too, to suppose that Mesmerism can be used at will to strike down victims, helpless and unconscious, as laudanum does, except in cases of excessive suscep-tibility from disease; cases which are, of course, under proper ward. The concurrence of two parties is needful in the first place, which is not the case in the administra-tion of narcotics; and then the practice is very uncer-tain in its results on most single occasions; and again, in the majority of instances, it appears that the intel-lectual and moral powers are more, and not less, vigor-ous than in the ordinary state. As far as I have any means of judging, the highest faculties are seen in their utmost perfection during the mesmeric sleep; the inno-

cent are stronger in their rectitude than ever, rebuking
levity, reproving falsehood and flattery, and indignantly
refusing to tell secrets, or say or do anything they
ought not; while the more faulty then confess their
sins, and grieve over and ask pardon for their offences.
The volitions of the Mesmerist may actuate the movements of the patient's limbs, and suggest the material
of his ideas; but they seem unable to touch his *morale*.
In this state the *morale* appears supreme, as it is rarely
found in the ordinary condition. If this view is mistaken, if it is founded on too small a collection of facts,
let it be brought to the test and corrected. Let the
truth be ascertained and established; for it cannot be
extinguished, and it is too important to be neglected.

And now one word of respectful and sympathising
accost to those reverent and humble spirits who painfully question men's right to exercise faculties whose
scope is a new region of insight and foresight. They
ask whether to use these faculties be not to encroach
on holy ground, to trespass on the precincts of the
future and higher life. May I inquire of these, in
reply, what they conceive to be the divinely appointed
boundary of our knowledge and our powers? Can
they establish, or indicate, any other boundary than
the limit of the knowledge and powers themselves?
Has not the attempt to do so failed from age to age?
Is it not the most remarkable feature of the progress
of Time that, in handing over the future into the past,
he transmutes its material, incessantly and without
pause, converting what truth was mysterious, fearful,
impious to glance at, into that which is safe, beautiful,
and beneficent to contemplate and use: a clearly consecrated gift from the Father of all to the children
who seek the light of his countenance? Where is
his pleasure to be ascertained but in the ascertain-
ment of what he gives and permits, in the proof and
verification of what powers he has bestowed on us,
and what knowledge he has placed within our reach?

While regarding with shame all pride of intellect, and with fear the presumption of ignorance, I deeply feel that the truest humility is evinced by those who most simply accept and use the talents placed in their hands; and that the most childlike dependence upon the Creator appears in those who fearlessly apply the knowledge he discloses to the furtherance of that great consecrated object, the welfare of the family of man.

HARRIET MARTINEAU.

APPENDIX.

"I have said nothing of Phrenology," &c.—Page 38.

SINCE these Letters were written, phenomena have presented themselves which leave no more possible doubt in the minds of witnesses of the truth of Phrenology than of that of Mesmerism. As I wish to leave to the Letters their original character of first impressions, I insert here the observations which are necessary, in order to be just to Phrenology: and I shall give no more than are necessary to this object, because I wish to reserve for study the bulk of the new appearances which have presented themselves.

By degrees, as her Mesmerist became more experienced, J. manifested the passions and emotions, and expressed the kinds of ideas excited by touching the best-ascertained organs of the brain. Nothing can be conceived more beautiful than her countenance and gestures when Veneration, Benevolence, Ideality, and Hope are made active; nor more ludicrous than Destructiveness in so mild and affectionate a personage;— nor more disagreeable than her descent from her higher moods, when Self-esteem and Love of Approbation are excited, and made to take the direction of care for her dress and appearance. But these appearances cannot be conveyed by description or assertion. I will give facts.

On Saturday evening, Dec. 22d, when she was deep in the trance, and therefore abundant in manifestations,

a lady present took a sudden fancy to speak to her in
French,—when she instantly, and, as it were, mechani-
cally, repeated in English what was said. This startled
all present—(four persons)—for we knew that this girl
had never been taught any language. The experiment
was repeated again and again, and always with the
same result. The finger of the Mesmerist was then on
Imitation. When it was shifted to Language, J. did
not repeat what was said, but replied to it. The lady
and a physician present then spoke repeatedly in Italian;
and with the same results, according as the one or the
other organ was touched ; and then Dr. —— spoke to
her in German,—still with the same result.

The whole party did at first look aghast. When we
came to reflect, however, how often she had replied to
our thoughts, without the intervention of any language
whatever, it seemed no more wonderful that she should
read off our minds through languages which were un-
known to her. It is indeed clear that, provided the
ideas conveyed are within her scope, it matters nothing
in what language they are uttered. She has only once
since been deep enough for a repetition of this striking
act : and that was on the next Friday, when she again
replied to questions in French and German, put to her
by a lady and gentleman present.

One evening, her Mesmerist touched at once Caution
and Language, to see which would prevail,—whether
she would be silent or yield to the enforcement to speak.
The struggle was obvious ; and it ended curiously. She
put up her own hand to Firmness : and by this rein-
forcement of Caution, was enabled to keep silence.

When very deep, and active accordingly, and left
alone to do what she likes, her predominant affections
and emotions are of the purest kind, and most beauti-
fully manifested, so as to inspire feelings of reverence in
all who see her. Her attachment to her Mesmerist,
and to a lady who is a patient of this kind Mesmerist,
is strong, and, as freed from all conventional restraints

of expression, extremely interesting. One evening lately, when very happy, she drew near to these two ladies, put her arms about them, laid her head on their shoulders, and said, with a voice and countenance of affection and joy never to be forgotten, " We are one," —-and the ladies felt that the honour rested with them.

While Mrs. ———— was being mesmerised, late one evening, when J. was deep and happy in the trance, and leaning near, to catch what she could of the influence, the other patient tranquilly observed, (with eyes closed as fast as J.'s), " How beautiful *that* is !"

" What is beautiful ?" asked the Mesmerist.

" The bright light streaming from all your fingers."

" O !" said J., " do you only now see that ? I have been watching it all this while."

I had often read and heard of " the fluid being seen" by somnambules. Mrs. ———— was not asleep, and this was the first occasion on which J. had spoken of the appearance.

I may now qualify what I said in the letters of J. being unable to tell anything concerning any stranger. As her powers improve, she becomes able—on rare occasions, which can never be anticipated—to discern, bit by bit, the disease of a person she never heard of, whose hair, sent under proper conditions, is silently put into her hands. This exercise appears to absorb her attention and interest more than any other. She renews the effort, time after time, sees more and more, and in one case appears to have penetrated the matter completely, declaring spontaneously, that the lady (whom she could never have heard of, and who is a stranger to us) was nearly blind, and must be treated in such and such a manner.

The scientific gentlemen who have watched this case, are most interested by the experiments with metals, as the most exact and nearly invariable. We have a persuasion that this is the avenue through which lies the most safe and direct path to a true theory of

Mesmerism.   We are in possession of a good many facts under this head ; but it is better to reserve them.   I will only give the remark of a gentleman on the invariable spectacle of a somnambule throwing away steel, however firmly grasped before, the moment it is touched with gold,—and usually with complaints of being burnt. This gentleman observed how many conditions are requisite to a fair trial of mesmeric experiments, and how careless novices are of them,—pointing out how the shrinking of the muscles of entranced patients under surgical operations may happen, in consistency with their unconsciousness of the pain,—the instruments being all made of steel, and the operator having probably a gold ring on his finger, of whose agency in the experiment he never thinks.

The very preparation for philosophical experimenting is hardly begun, except among an exceedingly small number of trained observers.

TYNEMOUTH,
    January 4. 1845

THE END.

LONDON :
BRADBURY AND EVANS, PRINTERS, WHITFFRIARS.

MEDICAL REPORT

OF THE

CASE OF MISS H—— M——.

MEDICAL REPORT

OF

THE CASE OF MISS H— M—.

BY T. M. GREENHOW,

FELLOW OF THE ROYAL COLLEGE OF SURGEONS OF ENGLAND ;
SENIOR SURGEON TO THE NEWCASTLE-UPON-TYNE INFIRMARY,
AND EYE INFIRMARY.

LONDON:

SAMUEL HIGHLEY, 32, FLEET STREET.

E. CHARNLEY, NEWCASTLE.

1845.

LONDON:
Printed by S. & J. BENTLEY, WILSON, and FLEY,
Bangor House, Shoe Lane.

PREFACE.

THE publication of the following case is forced upon me, in some degree, by the general interest which it has excited, but, especially by the misapprehensions which have arisen and been extensively circulated through the medical and other journals, respecting the correctness of the opinion I had entertained of its nature, and the treatment pursued for its relief.

In laying a full, but concise history of it before the profession, I need scarcely declare that I have the entire concurrence of the patient; whose high sense of duty both to other sufferers from similar disease, and to myself, as her medical attendant, during the long period of her confinement as an invalid, enables her to lay aside

those feelings of false delicacy which might have
led many, of less firmness of purpose, to shrink
from the explanation of the precise causes of such
continued suffering, although, scarcely any one
was ignorant of their general character.

How far the relief from the sympathetic nervous distress, attendant on this case, is to be attributed to the direct agency of mesmerism—
whether it has acted by a power *sui generis,*
or by supplying a powerful and well-timed stimulus to the mind, and thus acting through the
imagination and the will, is a question which
every one must be left to answer for himself,
after a careful consideration of the facts related
in the following pages and in the communications
to the *Athenæum,* lately supplied by the patient
herself.

The numerous and striking claims in favour of
mesmerism, emanating from so many sources,
have, at length, rendered it a subject of serious
and philosophical inquiry, which can no longer be
resisted by the members of the medical profession. It is by them only that its pretensions can

vii

be properly weighed — and it certainly behoves them to enter on the inquiry with candid and unprejudiced minds.

If there be such a power, careful investigation will, doubtless, enable them to detect it beyond dispute; and they will presently be prepared by the accumulation of facts, if not to determine its precise nature, at any rate, to ascertain its modes of operation and to define its capabilities and proper limits.

It is in this spirit of calm and dispassionate inquiry, that I have myself entered on the investigation, though I must admit that my efforts have not yet been attended with any results confirmatory of the powers of mesmerism; but I shall proceed circumspectly in my experiments, till repeated failures shall either confirm my doubts, or positive practical results remove them; in which case, I shall not fail to make such results known to the profession.

T. M. GREENHOW.

Newcastle-upon-Tyne,
Dec. 14, 1844.

CASE.

In a letter from Venice, dated June 14th, 1839, Miss H. M., æt. 37, first communicated to me her early feelings of indisposition. During the preceding year she had been sensible of a " great failure of nerve and spirits, and of strength." Frequently she experienced sharp pain in the uterine region. The Catamenia became more frequent, occurring every two or three weeks; and a very irritating discharge, of a brown or yellowish colour, took place in the intervals.

The irregular uterine discharges continued, occasionally mixed with clotted blood, and she suffered from many distressing nervous symptoms, evidently arising from uterine irritation; " inability to stand or walk, aching and weariness of the back, extending down the legs to the heels;" " tenderness and pain, on pressure, in the left groin, extending by the hip to the back. The spirits became much depressed, and the

B

power of enjoyment was gone." At the same time, " a *membranous substance*, like the end of a little finger," was discovered projecting from the os uteri.

This substance is described in the following terms, in a letter to Dr. Nardo, of Venice, who was consulted on the occasion, by a friend who accompanied Miss H. M. on her journey. " Twice there has been a discharge similar in colour and substance to blood. Two days ago it was found, that from the same passage (vagina) was protruding the extremity of a solid substance, totally insensible, of a reddish-brown colour, in form resembling the end of a bullock's tongue, with a decided edge or point—it can be pushed back without difficulty or pain, but it falls again." Dr. Nardo, who had no opportunity of actual examination, conjectured either Prolapsus Uteri or a Polypus tumour, of a fibrous nature, to be the occasion of these appearances; and recommended the careful avoidance of violent motion, and all that was found to increase indisposition.

The following extract from a letter, dated Lucerne, July 6, 1839, seems to fix the period when one character of the complaint, which will be presently noticed more particularly *(Retroversion of the Uterus),* took place:—" I cannot walk without injury, as I said, and keep my feet laid up, and my knees somewhat raised, as the easiest posture. I began to use the syringe, as you and Dr. Nardo recommended: it was a great relief, but in *three days* there was *no room for it*, and on this account I have never been able to use it since. I discontinued the sponge, finding it irritating, as you say, and it is not now *necessary*."

The use of the sponge as a pessary, and the syringe for injecting tepid water, or other fluid, into the vagina, is referred to in this passage, and needs no comment; it is the occupation of the cavity of the vagina by the enlarged and retroverted uterus, which I wish to be held in view, as throwing some light on the subsequent history of the case.

In the end of July, 1839, Miss H. M. arrived in Newcastle, and placed herself under my care. She was then suffering from the various morbid nervous sensations already described; and though she continued to take moderate walking exercise, it was attended with great discomfort and inconvenience. There was no difficulty in referring the whole train of symptoms to some organic or functional derangement of the uterus: and an examination was soon instituted to ascertain its proper character.

The uterus was found large, retroverted, and fixed low down in the vagina, the os and cervix uteri occupying the anterior part of the cavity, and the body and fundus of the organ passing horizontally backwards, till the latter approached the sacrum. The enlarged uterus thus occupying the antero-posterior diameter of the pelvis, pressed, respectively, against the urethra and neck of the bladder and the lower part of the rectum; and the embarrassment occasioned by this pressure produced corresponding symptoms, which were often the occasion of great uneasiness and inconvenience. While the fundus uteri extended backwards towards the sacrum, the cervix was bent downwards behind the pubes, nearly at a right angle, and hanging from the lip was a small polypus, which was soon removed; but without any alleviation of symptoms. I was assured by my patient that the projecting body, which showed itself at Venice, was different from, and much larger than, this small polypus; and though the os uteri was not dilatable with the finger, and, from its preternatural position, was in a very unfavourable condition for the exclusion of any body contained within the uterus, I was for some time led to hope that another and larger polypus might again make its appearance. Notwithstanding the use of suitable measures—warm baths and ergot of rye—to promote this object, my expectations were disappointed; and the treatment of the case soon resolved itself into the employment of appropriate palliatives.

The tenderness in the left groin was somewhat relieved by leeches. The increasing difficulty of bearing exercise, however moderate, soon rendered rest absolutely necessary; and the feelings of nervous discomfort indicated recourse to opiates, from which, though always used in great moderation, much relief was obtained. One of the most distressing symptoms which subsequently supervened, was an oppressive sickness, frequently amounting to retching; and much difficulty in micturition and in emptying the bowels was occasioned by the pressure of the uterine tumour. From the same cause arose the distressing pains down the lower extremities, frequently extending to the heels. The abdomen became considerably distended during the progress of these symptoms; but this arose more from a general distension and fulness of the bowels, from flatus and other contents, than the enlargement of the uterus, which could never be felt rising above the brim of the pelvis: though its increased size, doubtless, by pushing the abdominal viscera upwards,

14

tended in some measure to produce a general enlargement of the figure.

It not unfrequently happened, although, by the use of gentle aperients or emollient injections, a pretty regular action of the bowels was secured, that a gradual accumulation of their contents took place, giving rise to increased distress; which required the use of more active purgatives for its relief. An occasional attack of more acute disease from accidental causes—for example, a large abscess in the throat, or severe gastrodynia (from which Miss M. suffered long and acutely many years ago), was superadded to the ordinary symptoms arising from the local disease, aggravating their intensity, and leaving for a time the feeling of increased debility and inaptitude for physical exertion. The constant and distressing aching in the back rendered it painful to rest upon the sacrum in reclining on the sofa; and some relief was obtained by resting in a prone position. A couch, contrived for this purpose, was found a source of much comfort to the patient.

So little variation took place in the character of the symptoms, or the pathological condition of the affected organ, as to render needless minute details of continued morbid feelings, or of the treatment suggested for their relief.

15

In 1840 I made a statement of the case in writing to Sir Charles M. Clarke, who concurred with me in thinking that rest and palliative treatment, the general health being carefully maintained, could alone be depended upon.

In September, 1841, Sir Charles M. Clarke having occasion to visit this part of the country, I had an opportunity of availing myself more directly of his opinion.

After a very careful investigation of the case, Sir Charles gave an opinion verbally, which I was induced afterwards to request him to express in writing. In a note dated September 30th, 1841, he says,—" It was my intention to say that I perfectly agreed with you as to the nature of the complaint, that the Disease was an enlargement of the BODY of the Uterus; that the NECK of that organ was perfectly healthy; that although the majority of these cases of enlargement of the BODY of the uterus did not yield to external applications or to internal remedies, that, nevertheless, the disorder produced mechanical symptoms only, and *did not lead to any fatal result*, to which termination Disease of the *Neck* of the Uterus did lead.

" Farther, I mentioned that in an instance or two I *had* known such complaints as Miss M.'s subside, and that I would suggest the employ-

ment of certain means for this desirable purpose."
The means proposed by Sir Charles M. Clarke
was the continued external use of Iodine Oint-
ment.

To this measure my patient had so decided an
objection, that she could not be prevailed upon
to carry it into effect. It was on this account
that I was induced to propose a course of Iodide
of Iron, which, with few and short intervals, was
persevered in till July or August of the present
year. Under the use of this medicine the distressing sickness was greatly mitigated, the appetite improved, some morbid feelings were alle-
viated, and an increased tone of general bodily
health, as well as of mental energy, showed itself.
The following extract from a note written in
September, 1843, will show her own opinion of
its effects at that time:—" I suppose I owe my
much improved comfort mainly to them (the pills
of iodide of iron); indeed, it is very great. The
pulling and sinking—the mechanical troubles as
one may call them—of course continue, but the
almost total absence of sickness, and the striking
lessening of the ' distress' are such a comfort to
me!" Occasional, but not very frequent examinations took place into the pathological condition of the affected organ, but no appreciable
change could be discovered, except the appear-

ance of a membranous substance at the os uteri, which, generally, scarcely protruded beyond its lips, though occasionally it was described as of larger extent. This was said to resemble the appearance observed at Venice, though of smaller dimensions. This substance evidently proceeded from the interior of the uterus, and had no attachment to the neck, the point of the finger passing round it on all sides. Its appearance naturally gave rise to the renewed supposition that the uterus might contain a preternatural growth of a polypus character, the separation and discharge of which might be effected by time.

On the 2nd of April, 1844, I was first enabled to detect a slight change in the condition of the uterus. The attachment of the fundus was less fixed, and it could be slightly raised from its position. The membranous pendicle described above, and the general position of the organ, remained as on former examinations.

In the beginning of June, Miss M. suffered much from an attack of indigestion, with disordered and loaded bowels. The symptoms proper to the organic affection, especially the distressing pain in the back, were for a time increased; and while proper means were resorted to for the correction of visceral derangement, a Plaster with Belladonna was applied to the sacral region, from which but slight relief was obtained. The unwonted symptoms of indisposition had subsided, when, on June 22nd, the Mesmeric treatment was commenced, of which a full account has been published in the Athenæum by Miss M. From this time she ceased to be properly under my care, though her accustomed remedies were not yet laid aside. I shall therefore pass over the interval till September 4th, on which day I carefully repeated my examination, and found, as on April 2nd, that the posterior connections of the uterus were less fixed than formerly. The retroversion continues, but the fundus, which rests against the rectum and sacrum, feels looser, and admits of being raised to some extent with the finger in vaginam.

The uterus feels altogether less firm, and more yielding in its substance, and the os uteri is to a certain extent dilatable, yielding to the finger in a slight degree more than formerly. Within, and slightly projecting from the os uteri, can be felt *two* substances, which convey to the finger a sensation as if two lumbrici, of moderate size, hung through the mouth of the uterus. These membranous projecting bodies are said, on pressure, occasionally to exude a reddish discharge. In addition to the knowledge obtained by this examination, Miss M. supplied me with the fol-

lowing reports of herself, at this and several
succeeding visits which I made her, previous to
the next and final examination into the pathological condition of the uterus, on December 6th.
On this day, (September 4th,) she informed me
that the Catamenia which for many years had
taken place at shorter intervals than natural,
(every two or three weeks) have resumed their
natural course. That the breasts have increased
in bulk. The Pills of Iodide of Iron, and all
aperients, have been discontinued, the bowels
having lately acted with ease and regularity.
The use of opiates has been greatly diminished
by Enema, and internally, altogether omitted.
The sickness and other gastric inconveniences
have ceased; the irritation in the rectum and
neck of the bladder are no longer complained of;
—quietude and repose have succeeded to rest-
lessness and irritability; and the nervous system
has acquired a greatly improved tone.

11th.—Miss M. continues comfortable, with
greatly diminished doses of the opiate; other
medicines unnecessary. Has this day been in
the garden for some time laid on a sofa cushion.

21st.—Miss M. reports favourably in all respects of herself. Opiate reduced to a very
small dose. Yesterday walked round the Castle
yard; to-day, the same, with the addition of a

walk to the Haven — feels somewhat tired, but no other uneasy effects.

October 8th.—Miss M. informed me that she can now take long walks—to-day, two miles and a half. Has discontinued opiates for five days. At first the nights were bad. Last night she slept well, having taken a small quantity of warm brandy and water. No irritation is now felt at the neck of the bladder. Some pressure still on rectum, but otherwise feels well. Bowels regular without medicine.

December 6.—Again I made a careful examination into the state of Miss M. The fundus uteri is more disengaged than at the last examination, and admits of being raised somewhat higher. It is certainly *less fixed*, and in this respect has improved at each time of examination since April 2nd, when the first degree of improvement was observed. The retroversion continues, the fundus still extending towards the sacrum, while the os uteri approaches the pubes—the organ remains large and firm, and is yet turned back nearly at a right angle from the cervix uteri. The two membranous pendicles remain hanging out of the os uteri, as at the last examination. The health is represented as quite good, and the catamenia as regular—the nervous pains and irritations having all subsided. The person is less but, as abdominal distension depended principally upon the gaseous and other contents of the intestines, and in a slight degree only, on the uterine tumour, it is probable that renewed habits of activity have greatly contributed to restore the symmetry of the person in this respect.

I have purposely avoided interrupting the narrative of the case by details of the medicines prescribed. But I shall here append the prescriptions employed, except on particular emergencies, during the last three years. A glance at them will suffice to show how erroneous is the supposition entertained by many persons that Miss M. was in the habit of seeking relief in large and unmeasured doses of opium.

1. Anodyne Lotion.
R Misturæ Camphoræ.
Mist. G. Acaciæ, āā ℥viii.
Tincturæ Opii. ℨvii. M.
One ounce to be injected into the rectum every alternate day.

2. Anodyne Pills.
R Pilulæ Rhei. co. gr. xviii.
Mur. Morphiæ, gr. iii. M. et divide in Pilul. xii.
One anodyne pill to be taken every alternate day, and occasionally when suffering more than ordinary distress.

3. Aperient Pills.
R Ext. Colocynth. co.
Ext. Hyoseyami, āā ℨi. M. et divide in Pilul. xxiv.
Two aperient pills to be taken every alternate night, between the use of the anodyne injection.

4. Tonic Pills.

R Ferri. Iodidi.

Pulv. Zingib. āā gr. xxx, Cons. q. s. ut ft. Pilul. xxx.

One tonic pill to be taken three times a day.

Before the use of the anodyne lotion, it was occasionally found necessary to empty the rectum, by means of a common domestic injection.

I have endeavoured to render the preceding sketch comprehensive and concise, avoiding equally unnecessary details, and omitting nothing essential to the full comprehension of the true character of the case. Knowing well that no symptoms of malignant disease of the affected organ existed, I always believed that a time would arrive when my patient would be relieved from most of her distressing symptoms, and released from her long continued confinement. The catamenial crisis appeared the most probable period, but I did not despair of this happening sooner; though she never willingly listened to my suggestions of the probability of such prospective events, and seemed always best satisfied with anything approaching to an admission that she must ever remain a secluded invalid. This state of mind, perhaps, may be considered as an additional symptom of the morbid influence over the nervous system, of the class of diseases in which this case must be included.

During the last year or two, in common with many of the friends of Miss M., I had frequent opportunities of observing the increased ease and freedom with which she moved about her sitting-room ; and my conviction became confirmed, that the time was approaching when she would resume her habits of exercise in the open air. Oftener than once I have made use of the somewhat strong expression, that some day, probably before long, Miss M. *would take up her bed and walk.*

In the history of this case it is probable that the advocates of mesmerism will find reasons and arguments in support of their opinions. But the experienced practitioner, carefully distinguishing the *post hoc* from the *propter hoc*, will have little difficulty in bringing the whole into harmony with the well-established laws of human physiology.

As regards the pathology of the case, he will conclude that the condition of the uterus in December is but the natural sequel of progressive improvement begun in, or antecedent to, the month of April; and as regards the relief from the distressing nervous symptoms connected therewith, that the time had arrived when a new

24

and powerful stimulus only was required, to enable the enthusiastic mind of my patient to shake them off.

After bestowing my best consideration on the subject, this is the conclusion which most strongly forces itself on my own mind.

LONDON:
PRINTED BY S. & J. BENTLEY, WILSON, AND FLEY,
Bangor House, Shoe Lane.

www.ingramcontent.com/pod-product-compliance
Ingram Content Group UK Ltd.
Pitfield, Milton Keynes, MK11 3LW, UK
UKHW012337130625
459647UK00009B/342